HOW **DOGS** WORK

WRITTEN BY DANIEL TATARSKY
ILLUSTRATED BY DAVID HUMPHRIES

HOW DOGS WORK

A NOSE-TO-TAIL GUIDE TO YOUR CANINE

DK LONDON
Senior Editors Julie Ferris, Georgina Palffy
Senior Designer Amy Child
Designer Kit Lane
Managing Editors Fran Baines, Angeles Gavira
Managing Art Editors Michael Duffy, Phil Letsu
Production Editor Kavita Varma
Senior Production Controller Meskerem Berhane
Jacket Designer Surabhi Wadhwa
Publisher Liz Wheeler
Art Director Karen Self

First published in Great Britain in 2021 by Dorling Kindersley Limited
DK, One Embassy Gardens, 8 Viaduct Gardens,
London, SW11 7BW

The authorized representative in the EEA is
Dorling Kindersley Verlag GmbH. Arnulfstr. 124,
80636 Munich, Germany

Dorling Kindersley Limited
A Penguin Random House Company
10 9 8 7 6 5 4 3 2 1
001–322076–Sept/2021

A CIP catalogue record for this book
is available from the British Library.
ISBN: 978-0-2414-7119-7

Printed and bound in Slovakia

For the curious
www.dk.com

This book was made with Forest Stewardship Council ™ certified paper – one small step in DK's commitment to a sustainable future.

For more information go to www.dk.com/our-green-pledge

Contents

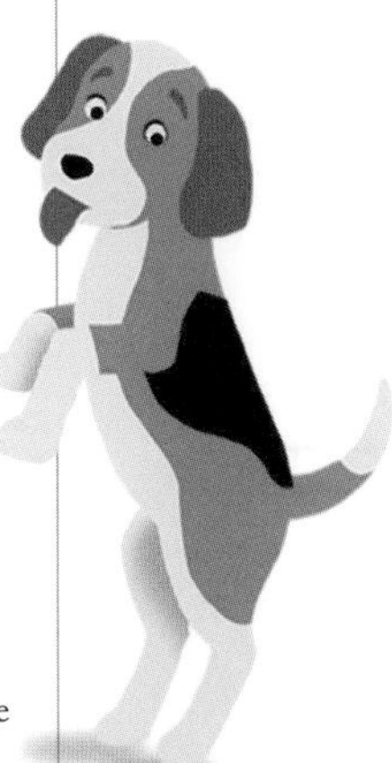

Introduction

When I was young, a long time ago, I didn't like dogs. I was afraid of them. If I saw one approaching me, my heart would race and I would try to avoid it. This all changed when Rooney, a Border Terrier, entered my life.

We call him Rooney but his kennel name is the rather grand Ottaswell Cador.

He was only eight weeks old and really tiny and I had to look after him. I hadn't thought about the fact that in looking after a dog, I would have to interact with other dogs. This started with socialization classes, which led on to taking him for walks and meeting every dog in the park! He was only a few months old and he wasn't afraid of them so how could I be?

Over those first few months, while I was getting used to living with a dog, I spent a lot of time watching him and, of course, playing with him. Everything was new for him and I began to see things through his eyes. A bouncing ball seemed alive when he played with it. A chase around the house was a big adventure. He loved it when I made up new games and never seemed to get tired or bored.

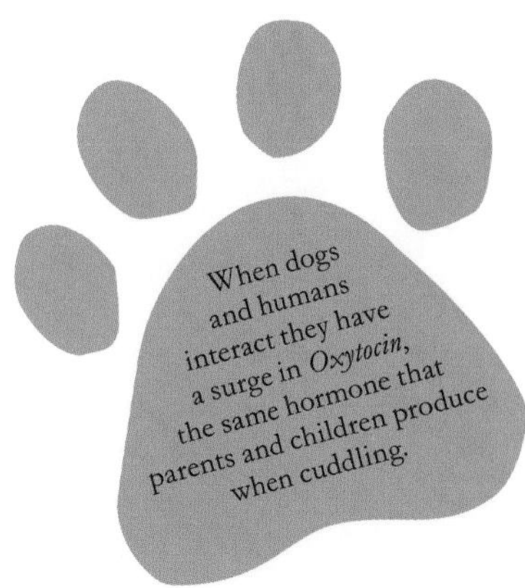

Teaching him even small things like stay or lie-down was rewarding for both of us. He wanted to learn and he wanted to make me smile almost as much as I wanted to see his tail wag. I like to think we brought the best out in each other.

There's a saying that you may hear a lot: "Be more dog". I think I know what it means now through living with Rooney. To sum it up in one sentence: live in the moment. He loves the thing he is doing at any instant, until he stops doing it and then he loves the next thing. And so on.

When I came up with the idea to write this book, which I would never have done without Rooney, I wanted it to be the sort of book a dog might like; if they had opposable thumbs and could read.

You can have fun or be intrigued by any page and then go somewhere else and enjoy that page. You don't have to read it from page one to the end. Jump around, waggle your tail, and look for the bits that make you laugh, make you think, or make you want to know more. Then go and do something else, walk your dog, and come back later.

Hopefully by the time you've seen every page you'll know *how dogs work* and much more, and maybe, just maybe, you can be more dog yourself.

From two came many

There is no other species on planet Earth with as wide a variation as the dog, so it is difficult to imagine that all dogs, from the Chihuahua to the Great Dane, evolved from wolves that would have all looked very similar, but this is the case.

Evolution

It was thought for a long time that dogs were the direct descendants of the grey wolves that we still see today. This belief has been overturned recently and it is now theorised that while they are related to our grey wolves, they are more like third cousins once removed. *Canus familiaris*, to give the domesticated dog its Latin name, is most likely to have ancestors who are now extinct. They were wolves, but the grey wolf we know is not their descendant.

The split from the wolf line happened some time between 20 and 40 thousand years ago, while the oldest discovered remains of a dog directly related to modern dogs has been dated from 14,500 years ago. This tells us where our dogs come from but it doesn't cover the other half of the story, which is how come there is a such a wide variety of dogs? The answer to that is domestication and the culprits are us. Yes, we did it.

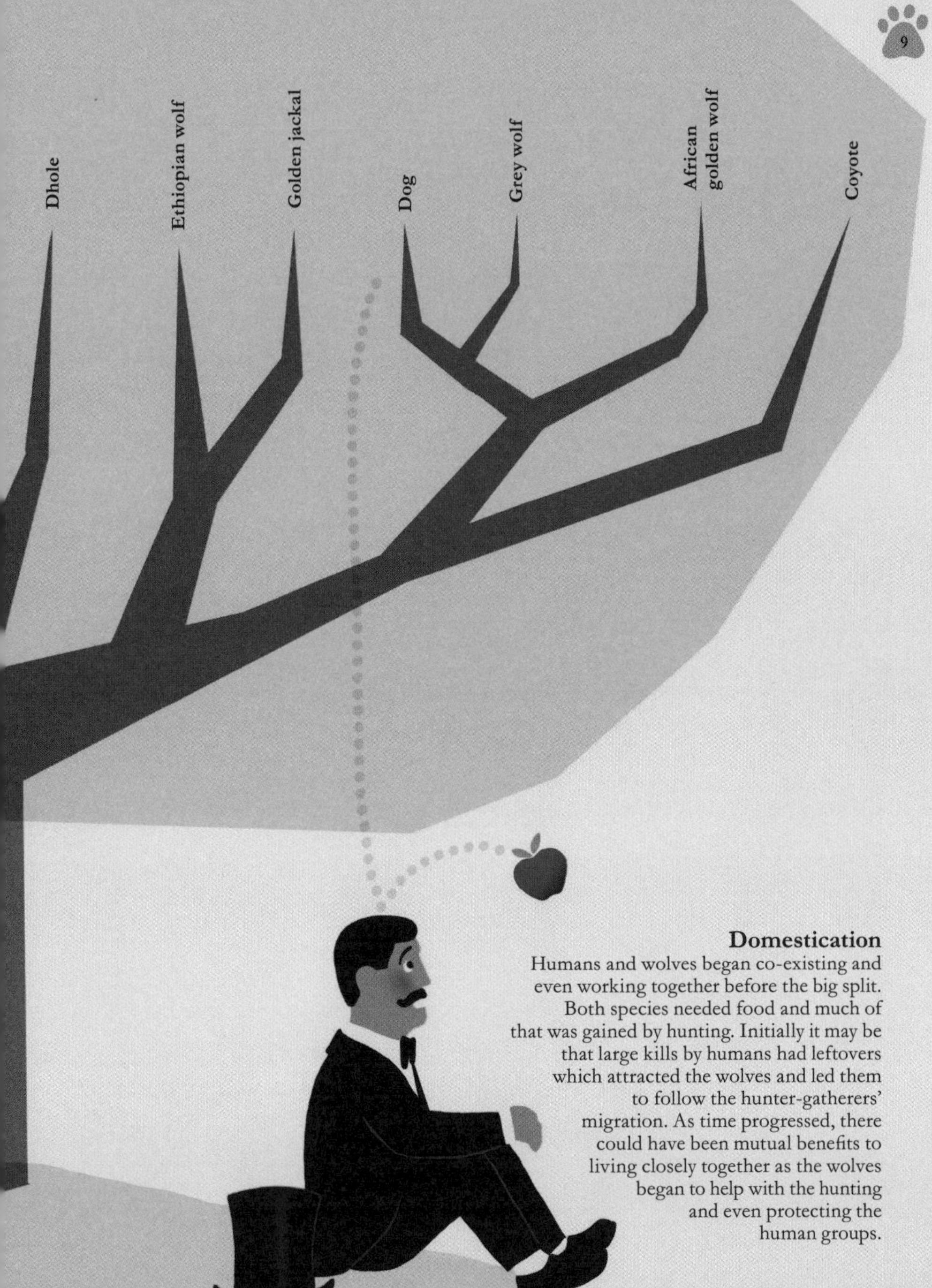

Domestication

Humans and wolves began co-existing and even working together before the big split. Both species needed food and much of that was gained by hunting. Initially it may be that large kills by humans had leftovers which attracted the wolves and led them to follow the hunter-gatherers' migration. As time progressed, there could have been mutual benefits to living closely together as the wolves began to help with the hunting and even protecting the human groups.

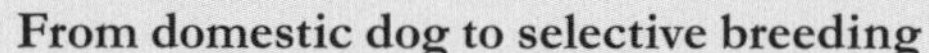

From domestic dog to selective breeding

When hunter-gatherers discovered agriculture these early dogs would no doubt have stayed with them as there was now a source of food on tap without the need to go hunting. Settlements sprang up around these prototype farms and everyone had a job to do. That last point is the vital one. When we say everyone had a job to do, that includes the dogs. Times were not so easy that you could have a dog as a pet, so it had to earn its keep and, like humans, each dog would have its own skills.

Victorian superbreeders

It was not until the Victorian era that selective breeding really took hold. The explosion of scientific thinking and experimentation along with a better understanding of evolution allowed, encouraged even, the Victorians to take breeding to its extreme extent.

Valuable skills

When certain skills were recognized as valuable, it was almost inevitable that the humans would step in to make sure that a useful dog would provide that service after it had died by passing on those traits to its offspring.

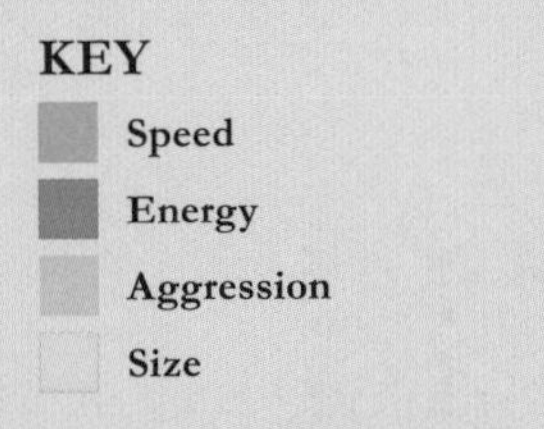

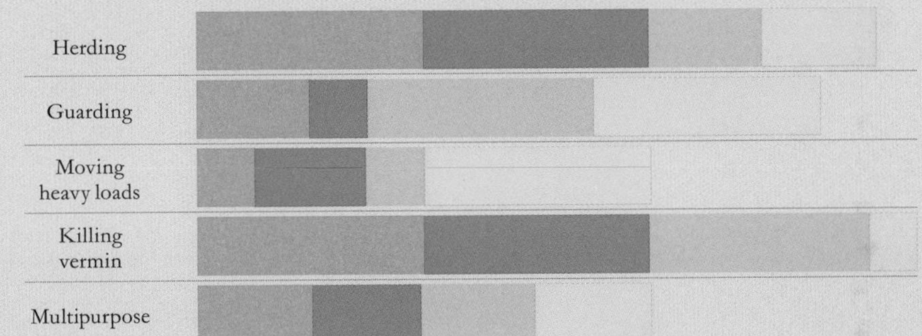

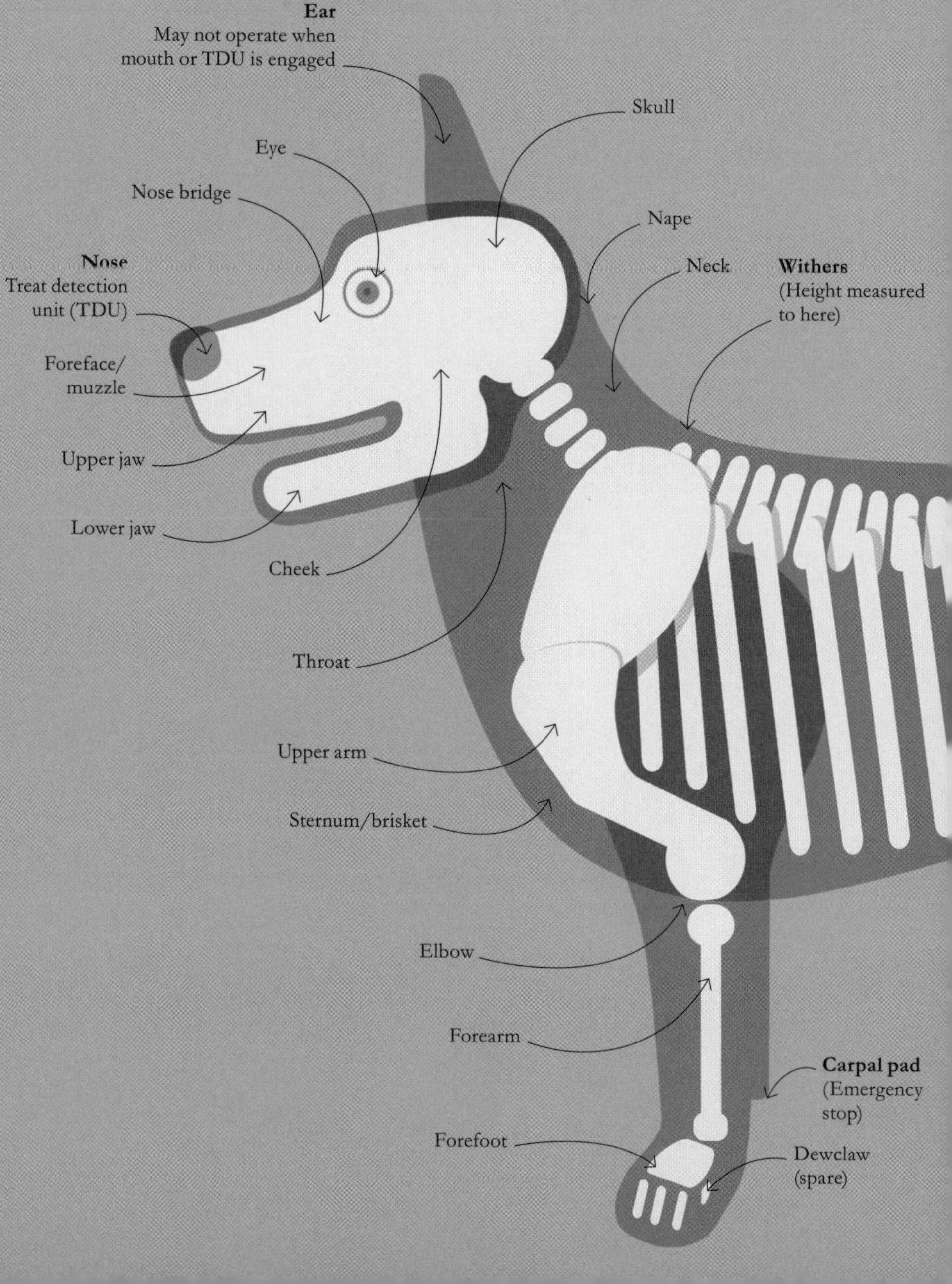

Ear
May not operate when mouth or TDU is engaged
Skull
Eye
Nose bridge
Nape
Nose
Treat detection unit (TDU)
Neck
Withers
(Height measured to here)
Foreface/ muzzle
Upper jaw
Lower jaw
Cheek
Throat
Upper arm
Sternum/brisket
Elbow
Forearm
Carpal pad
(Emergency stop)
Forefoot
Dewclaw (spare)

Basic dog anatomy

Much of the dog anatomy is quite obvious: nose, tail, eye, and so on, but a few of the terms are a total mystery to some. Here's a quick guide to what's what on a dog.

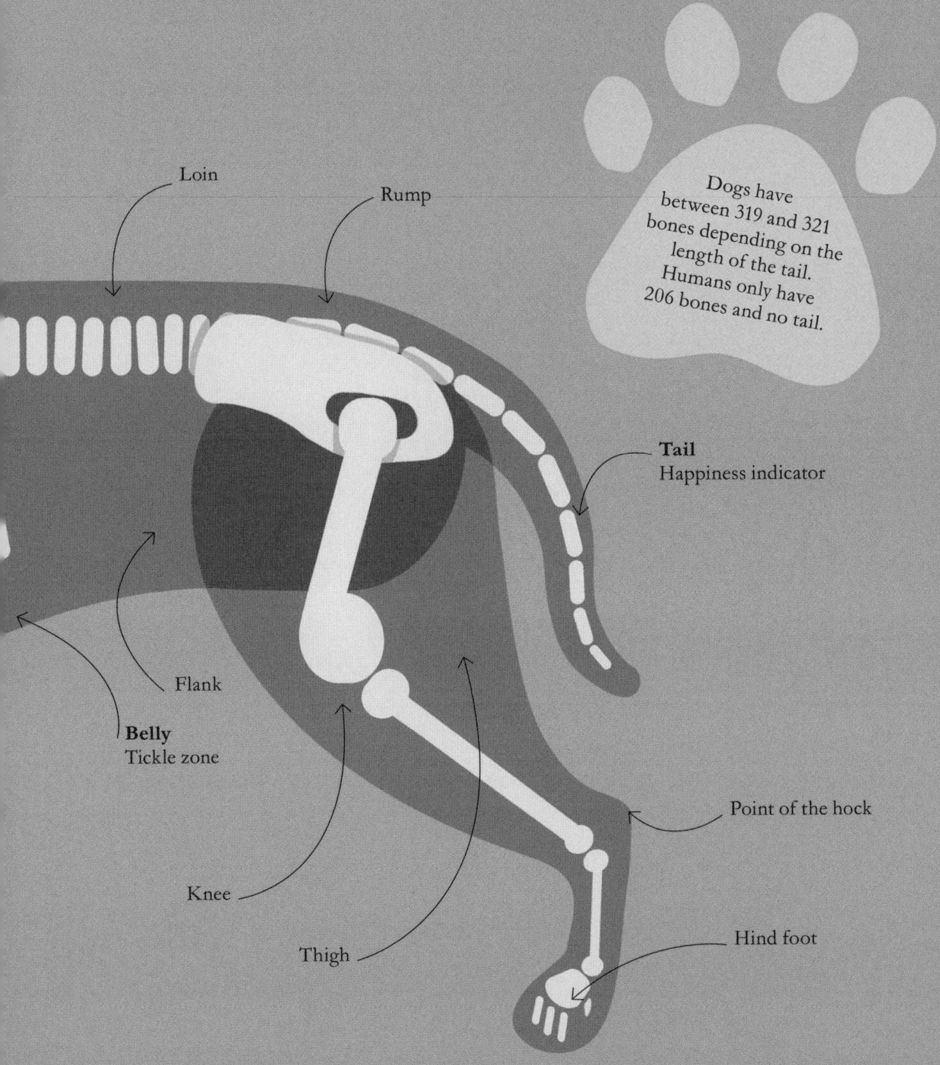

Dogs have between 319 and 321 bones depending on the length of the tail. Humans only have 206 bones and no tail.

Loin

Rump

Tail
Happiness indicator

Flank

Belly
Tickle zone

Point of the hock

Knee

Thigh

Hind foot

Body talk

The overall position of the dog's body has meaning. One reason dog owners need to be careful when approaching other dogs with a dog on a lead is that the lead can create a false impression of the dog's mood by making it stand at an unintended angle. If the owner holds the dog back, this changes a dog's posture from friendly to aggressive from the other dog's perspective.

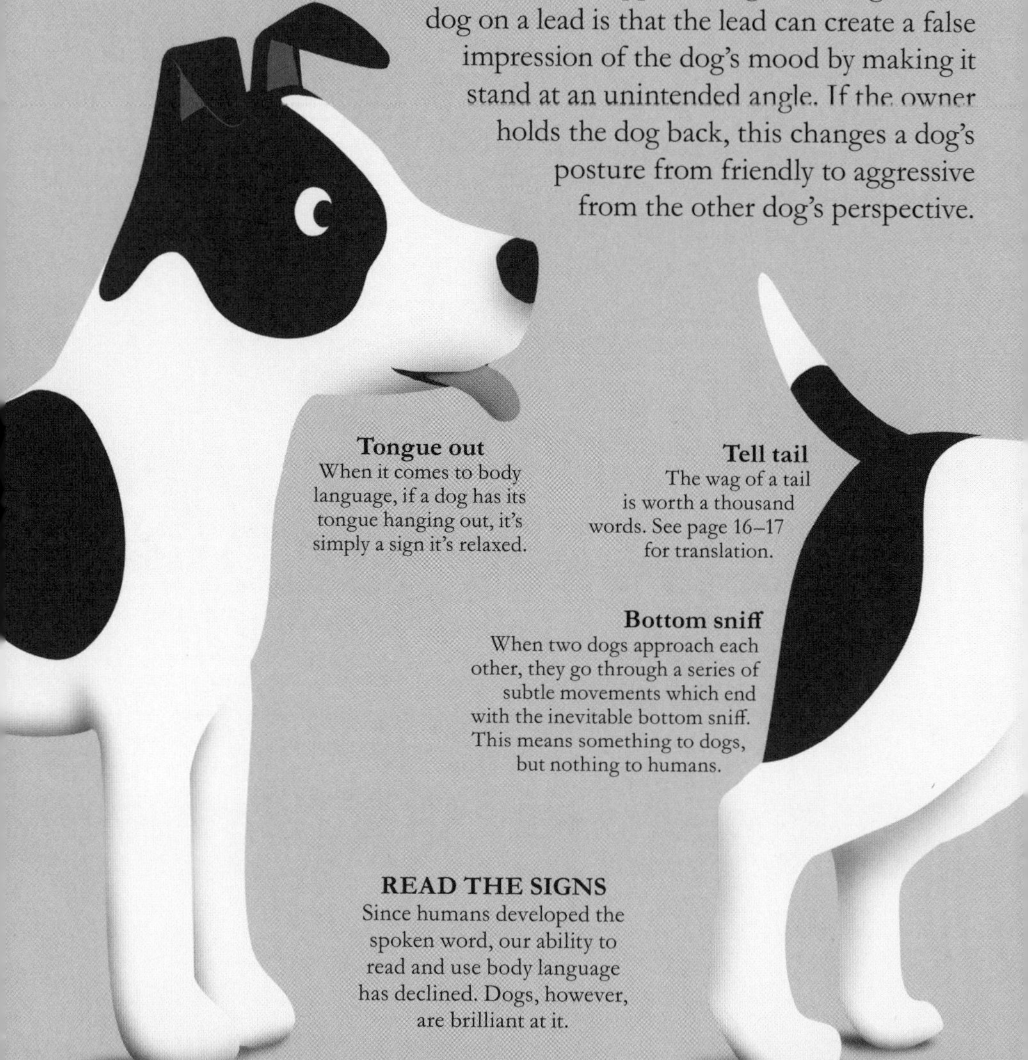

Tongue out
When it comes to body language, if a dog has its tongue hanging out, it's simply a sign it's relaxed.

Tell tail
The wag of a tail is worth a thousand words. See page 16–17 for translation.

Bottom sniff
When two dogs approach each other, they go through a series of subtle movements which end with the inevitable bottom sniff. This means something to dogs, but nothing to humans.

READ THE SIGNS
Since humans developed the spoken word, our ability to read and use body language has declined. Dogs, however, are brilliant at it.

Relaxed
Neutral, upright position

Alert, ready for action
Leaning forwards, weight on front legs, back sloping down towards tail

Eager, excited to play
Front legs splayed in front, back legs straight, tail wagging

Submissive
Lying on back as other dog approaches

Scared
Lying low, legs bent, tail curled under

World woofs
Italian dogs go "bau-bau!" French dogs "wouaff-wouaff!" Japanese dogs go "wan-wan!" Korean dogs "meong-meong!" Russian dogs go "gav-gav!" Except for very small ones, which go "tyav-tyav!"

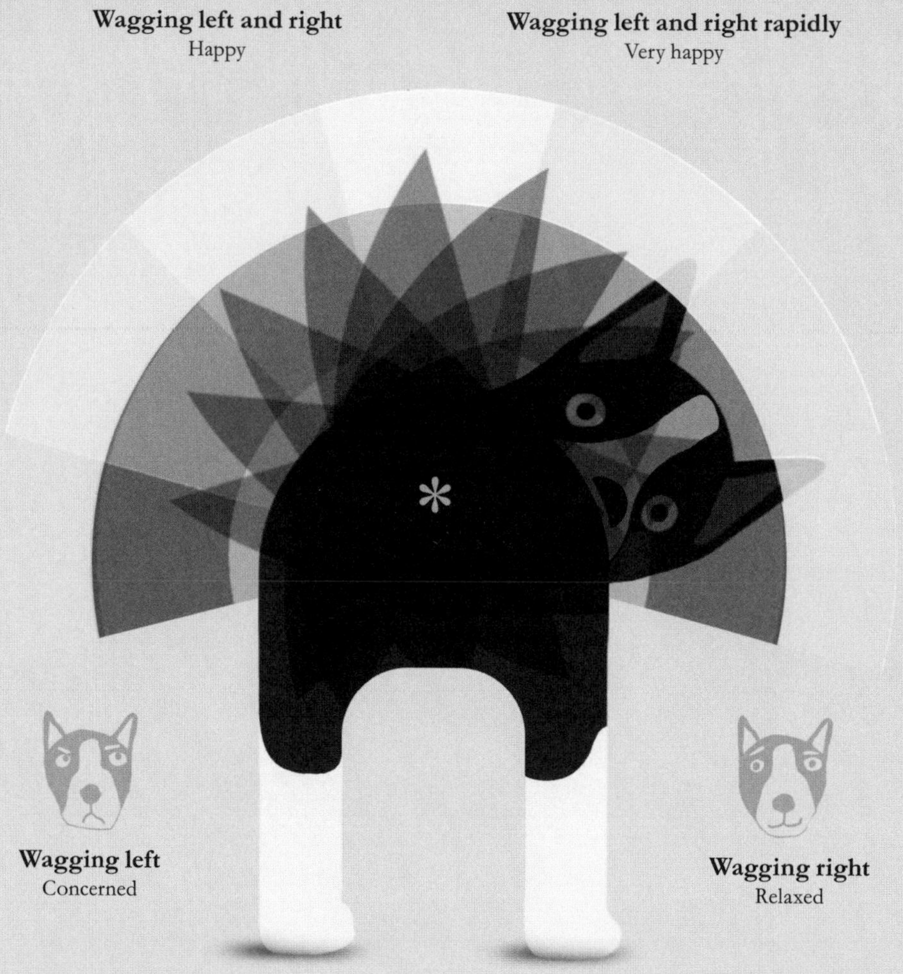

Telling tails

Everyone has a tale to tell and this is very true of the tell-tale dog's tail. Even if people know almost nothing about dogs the one thing they do know is that if it's wagging its tail, it's happy. But this curious appendage, which humans had, but lost many millennia ago, can tell us much more than that.

WAG-O-METER

This handy circular scale measures the angle of tail activity. Check your dog's rearguard action and work out where the tail lies on the chart to understand your dog's mood. It really is a shame that humans lost their tails.

All ears

Some breeds of dog can't really do much with their ears because they're so floppy, but others are positively verbose. There's mild debate about the head tilt. Some experts believe that when a dog tilts its head it's trying to see your whole face, but its snout is blocking the view. Others believe it is an attempt to clarify where a particular sound is coming from by moving the relative position of their ears. A final theory is that dogs know how incredibly cute they look when they do it.

Frightened
Flat and backwards:
scared, about to run away

Concerned
Up and sideways:
something's not quite right

Alert
Up and forwards:
not so friendly

Ready to attack
Flat and forwards:
really not a good sign

Twelve o'clock
Looking straight at you: you have my attention for the time being, so don't waste it.

One o'clock
Looking straight at you: you said something but I was thinking about lunch. Can you repeat it please?

Two o'clock
Looking straight at you: I heard it this time but I really didn't understand. One more time?

Two to ten o'clock
Looking straight at you: you're repeating the same thing and I don't know what you're saying. Can we just play chase?

Twelve o'clock
Looking down: I'm here but I'm not really interested in what you're saying. I could be sleeping.

Twelve o'clock
Looking above you: are we really going out with you wearing that hat? Seriously?

Pedigree dogs

Although distinct varieties of dog have been known for many hundreds of years, it is only since the mid-19th century that breed classifications have been formally recognized. Dog breeders formed clubs to agree standards for each breed, such as look and behaviour, and dogs that met the criteria became known as pedigree dogs.

If two pedigree dogs of the same breed have a puppy, their offspring is also a pedigree dog. For the puppy to be accepted as purebred, its parents need to be listed in a stud book and the new arrival has to be registered with a kennel club or other canine body. The oldest of these organizations is The Kennel Club (TKC), founded in 1873, which sets down consistent breed standards in the UK.

BREED GROUPS

This is how the kennel clubs group the breeds. TKC recognizes 221 breeds, the AKC has 197, while the FCI has a whopping 354. Woof woof!

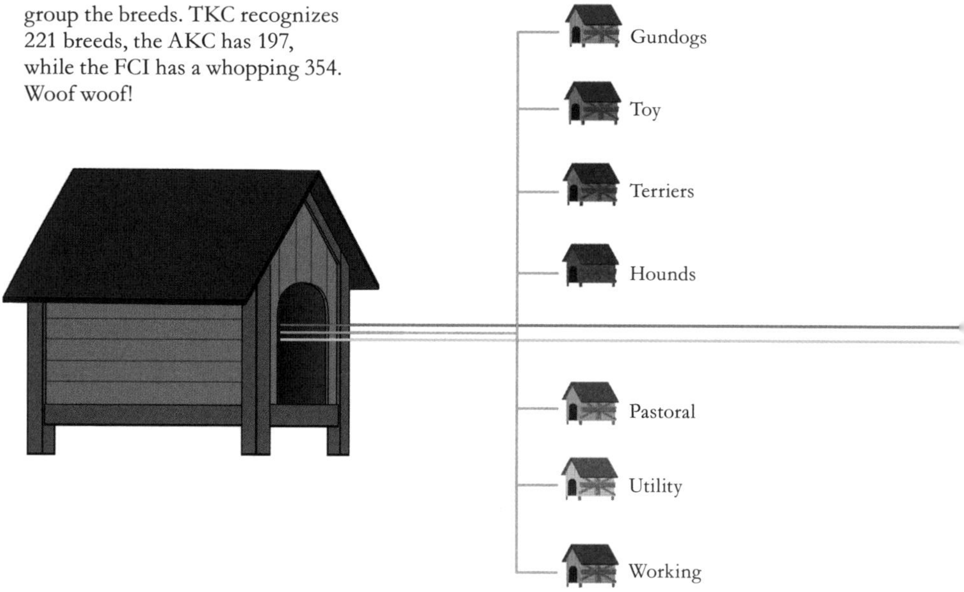

The Kennel Club

- Gundogs
- Toy
- Terriers
- Hounds
- Pastoral
- Utility
- Working

The American Kennel Club (AKC) regulates dog breeds in the US, while the Fédération Cynologique Internationale (World Canine Organization, FCI) represents the breeds of 98 member countries around the world.

The Kennel Club splits pedigree dogs into seven breed groups, as does the AKC – although they define the groups in different ways. The FCI, which recognizes more breeds overall, divides purebred dogs into 10 groups.

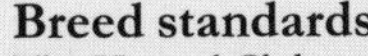

Breed standards

The Kennel Clubs set the benchmarks for breeders to follow to ensure consistency.

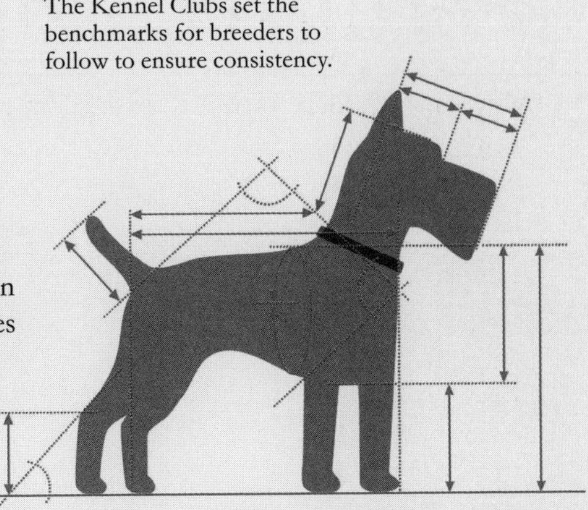

The American Kennel Club

- Sporting
- Toy
- Terriers
- Hounds
- Herding
- Non-sporting
- Working

Fédération Cynologique Internationale

- 7. Pointers
- 8. Retrievers, Flushing Dogs, and Water Dogs
- 9. Companion and Toy
- 3. Terriers
- 6. Scenthounds
- 10. Sighthounds
- 4. Dachshunds
- 1. Sheepdogs and Cattledogs
- 5. Spitz and Primitive Types
- 2. Pinscher and Schnauzer, Molossoid and Swiss, Mountain and Cattledogs

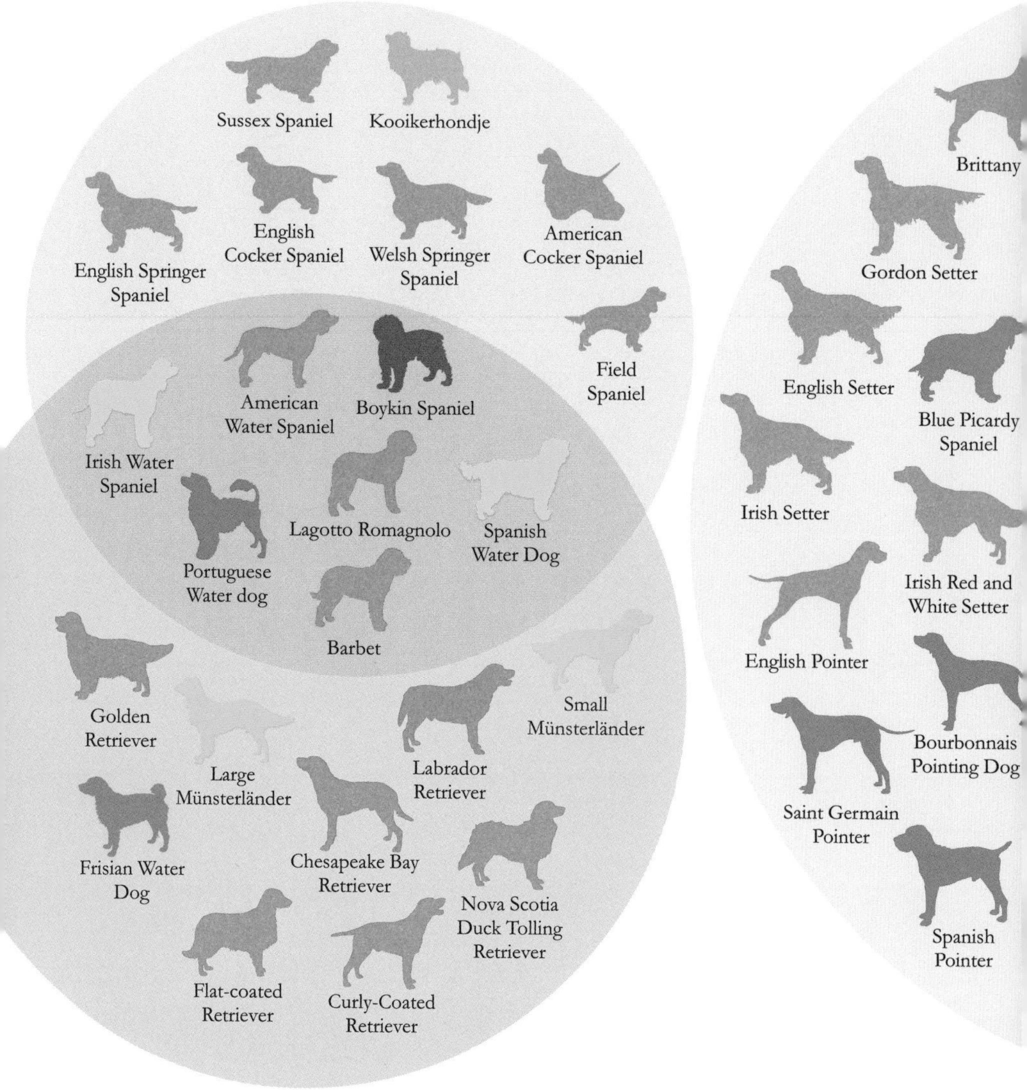

Sussex Spaniel

Kooikerhondje

English Springer Spaniel

English Cocker Spaniel

Welsh Springer Spaniel

American Cocker Spaniel

Field Spaniel

American Water Spaniel

Boykin Spaniel

Irish Water Spaniel

Portuguese Water dog

Lagotto Romagnolo

Spanish Water Dog

Barbet

Golden Retriever

Large Münsterländer

Labrador Retriever

Small Münsterländer

Frisian Water Dog

Chesapeake Bay Retriever

Nova Scotia Duck Tolling Retriever

Flat-coated Retriever

Curly-Coated Retriever

Brittany

Gordon Setter

English Setter

Blue Picardy Spaniel

Irish Setter

Irish Red and White Setter

English Pointer

Bourbonnais Pointing Dog

Saint Germain Pointer

Spanish Pointer

KENNEL CLASSIFICATIONS

The American Kennel Club refers to Gundogs as Sporting, while the FCI has simply split them into their individual functions across two groups: Pointing Dogs and Retrievers, Flushing and Water Dogs.

KEY

Dog type:

- Flusher
- Retriever
- Pointer
- Flusher and Retriever

Which clubs they belong to:

- American Kennel Club (AKC)
- Fédération Cynologique Internationale (FCI)
- AKC and FCI
- The Kennel Club (TKC) and FCI
- AKC, FCI, and TKC

Gundogs

Gundogs are bred for helping people hunt game, most usually birds, with guns! They find the birds, flush them out, and then bring them back once they have been shot. Most dogs specialize in one of these three roles, but some do all three. Pointers find the prey and stand motionless pointing towards the prey until the hunter or another dog flushes them out. Retrievers bring the game back without crushing it.

Gundogs as pets

Gundogs were bred to work all day so need lots of exercise. Good trainers, they work well with humans and are happy in most conditions. Since the 1970s, Gundogs have been the most popular group thanks to Retrievers (Labrador and Golden) and Spaniels (Cocker and English Springer). These have been regulars in the top breeds since the middle of the 1950s. Their popularity isn't because they are being used as Gundogs but because their characteristics make them the perfect family pet: easy to train, loyal, and friendly temperament.

Drentsche Partridge Dog

The Drentsche Partridge Dog is recognized by the FCI and AKC, but was only recognized by the TKC for a short period in the 1970s. The AKC actually has it in the Working group. Originating from the Drenthe area of the Netherlands, the Patrijshond can be seen in 17th-century paintings by Gabriël Metsu such as *Hunter Getting Dressed After Bathing*.

Cocker Spaniel

The Cocker Spaniel is the only breed to have featured in the UK's top ten for every decade since records began. The most famous member of the breed is probably Lady, of the Disney film *Lady and The Tramp*. There are two distinct but very similar Cocker Spaniels, the American and the English version. In their native countries both are simply called the Cocker Spaniel, whereas everywhere else they have their country's name included.

RETRIEVERS

One interesting thing to note is that as the Golden and Labrador Retriever have grown in popularity everywhere the Flat-Coated version has declined. Here's how they compare around the world.

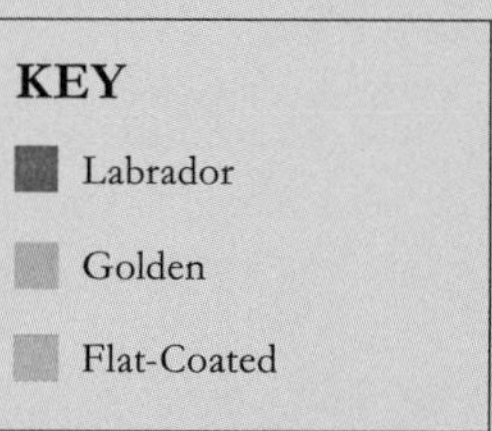

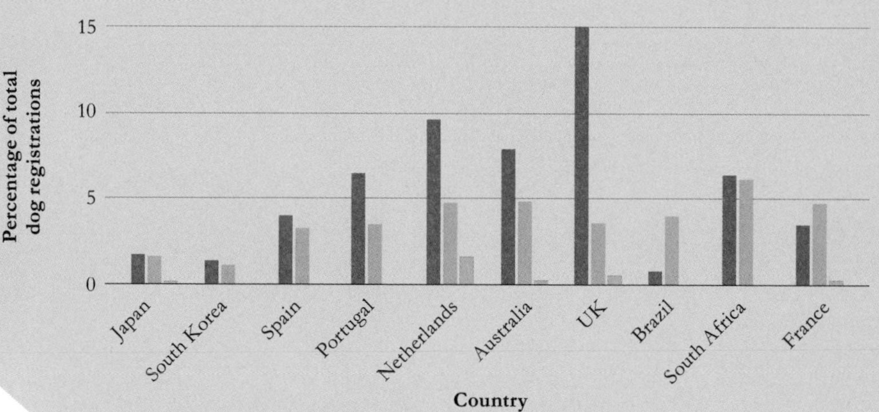

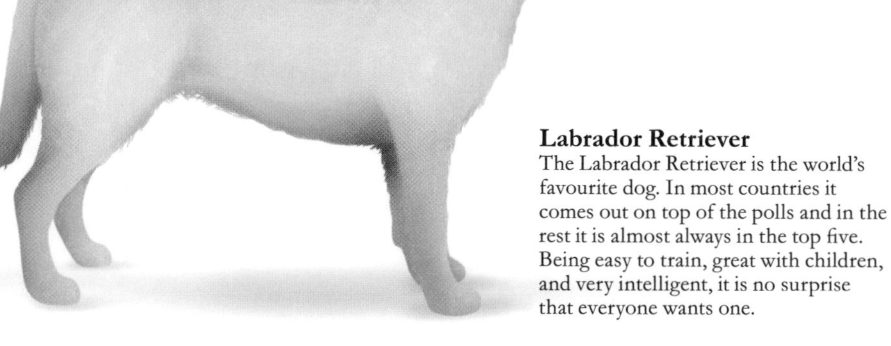

Labrador Retriever

The Labrador Retriever is the world's favourite dog. In most countries it comes out on top of the polls and in the rest it is almost always in the top five. Being easy to train, great with children, and very intelligent, it is no surprise that everyone wants one.

Famous dogs

American pop artist Andy Warhol is said to have said: "In the future, everyone will be world-famous for 15 minutes." It could be argued that this became true of Warhol's Dachshund. The artist took his dog everywhere and was often pictured with him. Archie's fame was by association, but here are some dogs who found the limelight through their own achievements.

KEY

The author has awarded each dog a star rating out of five for its celebrity, based on a range of criteria.

- **Fame** How well-known the dog is
- **Importance to Humanity** If the dog has aided human progress
- **Unprompted Recognition** Public awareness of their name
- **Appearance in Popular Culture** The dog's portrayal in all media
- **Star Quality** The dog's sheer animal magnetism and allure

Mongrel
(part-Samoyed Terrier)

LAIKA

A Muscovite street dog was the first living creature to orbit Earth. The Soviet Union's Sputnik 2 team used strays for the space mission as they believed that the dogs' lives had hardened them to extreme weather conditions. The rocket launched on 3 November 1957, but tragically Laika perished in flight. There is a statue of Laika at Russia's Training Centre for Cosmonauts.

Fame	★★★★★
Humanity	★★★★★
Recognition	★★★☆☆
Pop Culture	★★★★☆
Star Quality	★★★★☆

NIPPER

In 1899, English painter Francis Barraud completed a painting of Nipper looking quizzically into the horn of an Edison cylinder phonograph. Nipper had died four years earlier, and so never knew that his image was to become one of the best-known trademarks in the world. The painting, titled *His Master's Voice,* was used by record companies around the world.

Terrier mix

Fame
Humanity
Recognition
Pop Culture
Star Quality

ROBOT

Until 12 September 1940, the Lascaux caves in the Périgord region of France had lain undisturbed for 17,000 years. Today, the caves are famous worldwide for their prehistoric paintings, thanks to an accidental discovery by Robot. The dog fell down a hole while out walking with his owner, 18-year-old Marcel Ravidat, and three friends. When the four bipeds entered the caves in search of their four-legged friend they could not have imagined that they would find a treasure trove of Palaeolithic art.

Terrier mix

Fame
Humanity
Recognition
Pop Culture
Star Quality

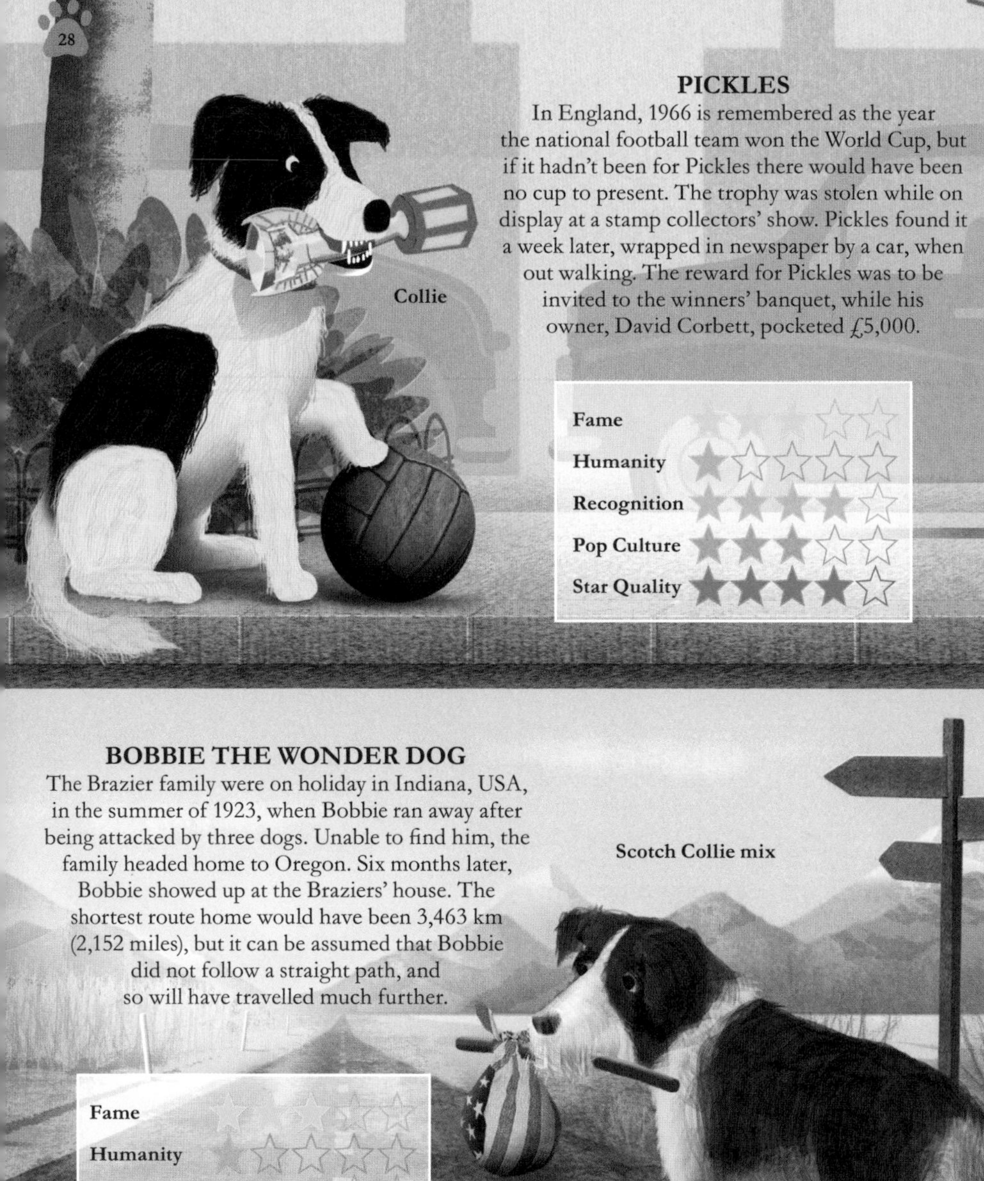

PICKLES

In England, 1966 is remembered as the year the national football team won the World Cup, but if it hadn't been for Pickles there would have been no cup to present. The trophy was stolen while on display at a stamp collectors' show. Pickles found it a week later, wrapped in newspaper by a car, when out walking. The reward for Pickles was to be invited to the winners' banquet, while his owner, David Corbett, pocketed £5,000.

Collie

Fame
Humanity
Recognition
Pop Culture
Star Quality

BOBBIE THE WONDER DOG

The Brazier family were on holiday in Indiana, USA, in the summer of 1923, when Bobbie ran away after being attacked by three dogs. Unable to find him, the family headed home to Oregon. Six months later, Bobbie showed up at the Braziers' house. The shortest route home would have been 3,463 km (2,152 miles), but it can be assumed that Bobbie did not follow a straight path, and so will have travelled much further.

Scotch Collie mix

Fame
Humanity
Recognition
Pop Culture
Star Quality

HACHIKŌ

In the 1920s, Japanese scientist Hidesaburō Ueno caught a train to work every day. His dog, Hachikō, would meet him at the station at the end of the day. When Ueno died, his faithful dog continued to wait for him at the station until his own demise 10 years later. Hachikō became a national symbol of loyalty. Each year, on the anniversary of his death, there is a ceremony at Shibuya station in Tokyo.

Akita Inu

Fame	★★★★★
Humanity	★★★★☆
Recognition	★★★★★
Pop Culture	★★★★☆
Star Quality	★★★★☆

TOP OF THE PUPS

Which of the famous dogs is most famous of all?

Sleeping
Dogs sleep on average for around eight hours through the night and nap for about four hours during the day. That's a lot of sleeping time!

Lounging
After your dog has exercised or eaten, you'll see them just lying around. Not asleep, but quite happily just lying around, for about seven hours a day.

Active
Some of your dog's level of activity will be reliant on what you do with them, but in an ideal world they do need to be on the go for around five hours a day.

REM

Non-REM

It's a dog's life

For the average pet pooch most of their time is spent doing pretty much nothing: roughly 80 per cent of every 24 hours involves sleeping or just lying around. What happens in the other five hours?

Do dogs dream?
The big question that keeps dog lovers awake is, "Do dogs dream?" Yes, of course they do. If you have a few minutes to spare, sit with your dog while they sleep. It won't be long before something twitches or they make a funny noise – involuntary actions caused by their dreams. You'll even see their tail wag when they dream of things that make them happy.

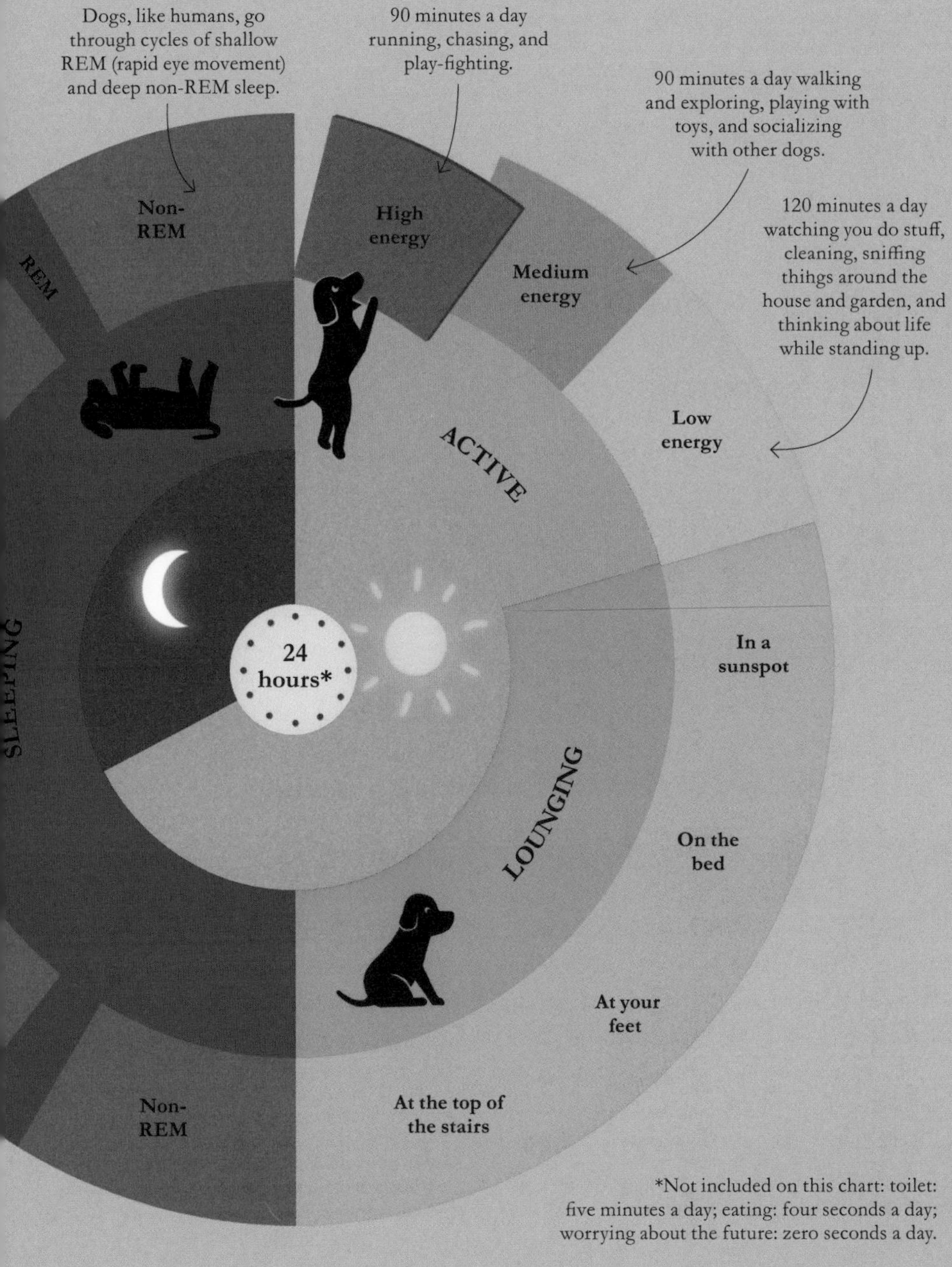
Dogs, like humans, go through cycles of shallow REM (rapid eye movement) and deep non-REM sleep.
90 minutes a day running, chasing, and play-fighting.
90 minutes a day walking and exploring, playing with toys, and socializing with other dogs.
120 minutes a day watching you do stuff, cleaning, sniffing things around the house and garden, and thinking about life while standing up.
Non-REM
REM
High energy
Medium energy
Low energy
ACTIVE
SLEEPING
24 hours*
LOUNGING
In a sunspot
On the bed
At your feet
At the top of the stairs
Non-REM

*Not included on this chart: toilet: five minutes a day; eating: four seconds a day; worrying about the future: zero seconds a day.

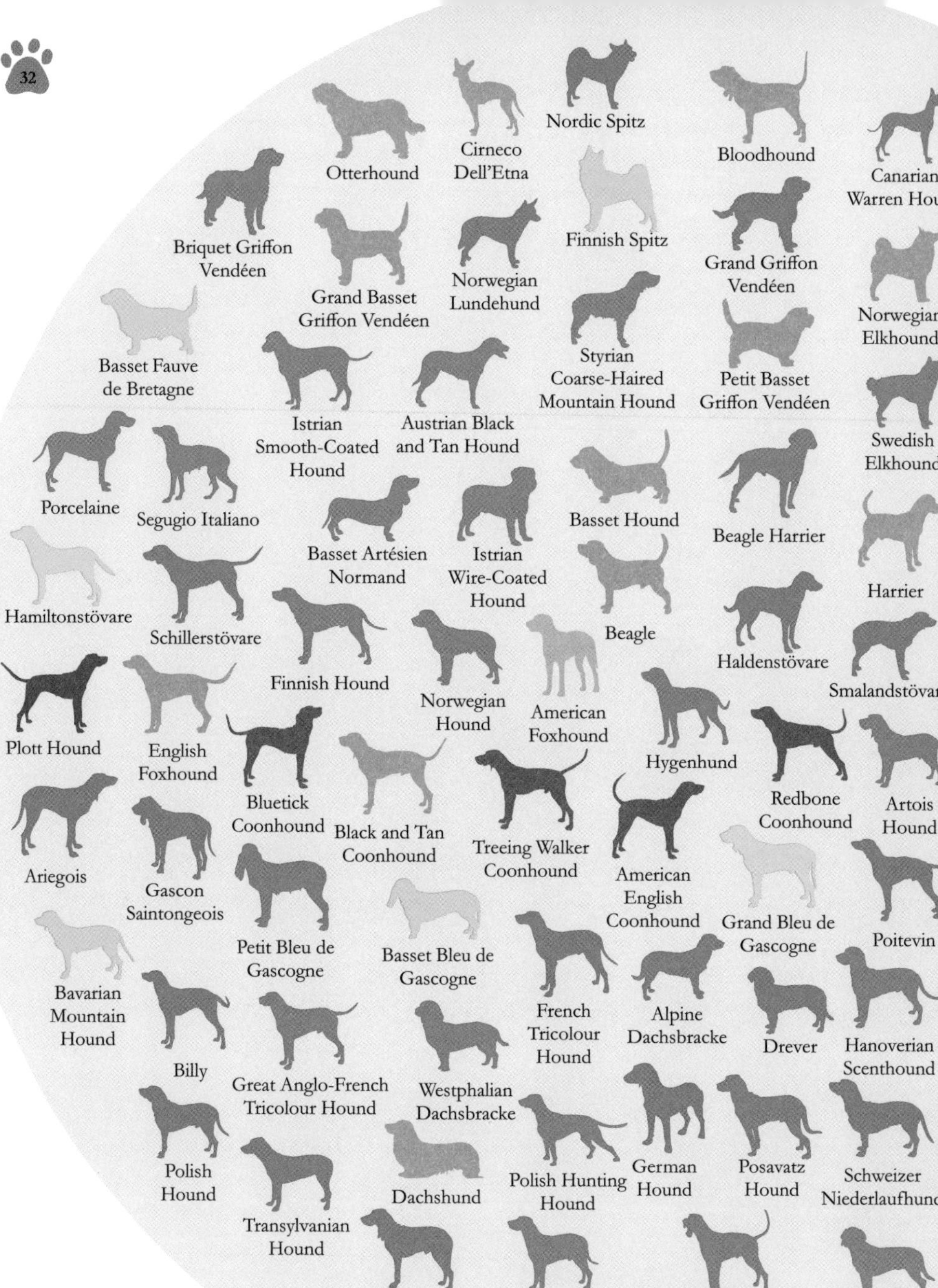
Otterhound
Cirneco Dell'Etna
Nordic Spitz
Bloodhound
Canarian Warren Houn
Briquet Griffon Vendéen
Grand Basset Griffon Vendéen
Norwegian Lundehund
Finnish Spitz
Grand Griffon Vendéen
Norwegian Elkhound
Basset Fauve de Bretagne
Istrian Smooth-Coated Hound
Austrian Black and Tan Hound
Styrian Coarse-Haired Mountain Hound
Petit Basset Griffon Vendéen
Swedish Elkhound
Porcelaine
Segugio Italiano
Basset Artésien Normand
Istrian Wire-Coated Hound
Basset Hound
Beagle Harrier
Harrier
Hamiltonstövare
Schillerstövare
Finnish Hound
Norwegian Hound
American Foxhound
Beagle
Haldenstövare
Smalandstövare
Plott Hound
English Foxhound
Bluetick Coonhound
Black and Tan Coonhound
Treeing Walker Coonhound
Hygenhund
Redbone Coonhound
Artois Hound
Ariegois
Gascon Saintongeois
Petit Bleu de Gascogne
Basset Bleu de Gascogne
American English Coonhound
Grand Bleu de Gascogne
Poitevin
Bavarian Mountain Hound
Billy
Great Anglo-French Tricolour Hound
Westphalian Dachsbracke
French Tricolour Hound
Alpine Dachsbracke
Drever
Hanoverian Scenthound
Polish Hound
Transylvanian Hound
Dachshund
Polish Hunting Hound
German Hound
Posavatz Hound
Schweizer Niederlaufhund
Schweizer Laufhund
Great Anglo-French Black and White Hound
French Black and White Hound
Slovakian Hound

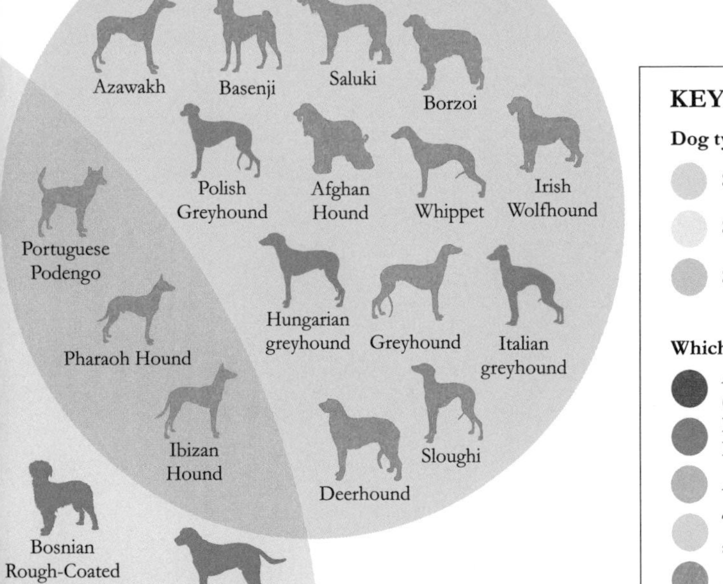

KEY

Dog type:

- Sighthound
- Scenthound
- Sight and scent

Which clubs they belong to:

- American Kennel Club (AKC)
- Fédération Cynologique Internationale (FCI)
- AKC and FCI
- The Kennel Club (TKC) and FCI
- AKC, FCI, and TKC

SIGHT AND SCENT

Hounds are split into two groups based on how they hunt: Sight and Scent. Sighthounds must be quick; they chase what they see so they need to keep it in sight. By contrast Scenthounds aren't necessarily speedy as they find their quarry by smell. They put the dog in dogged. There are a few hounds who combine the use of their eyes and nose!

Hounds

Like the Gundog group, the Hounds are hunters but there is one big difference: the Hounds do it quite naturally without any real training. The hunting instinct is in them and they do not generally wait for the command. If you see a dog chasing anything, from a squirrel to a deer, with its human bringing up the rear trying to gain control, there's a very good chance it will be a Hound.

DACHSHUND POPULARITY

Dachsuhunds are popular the world over as the table below shows. In the US, they are among the top 15 breeds and feature even higher up when looking at figures for city and apartment dwellers. Originally from Germany, they are also known as sausage dogs or wieners – German for sausage.

The figures in this graph cover all the varieties of Dachshund available in each country.

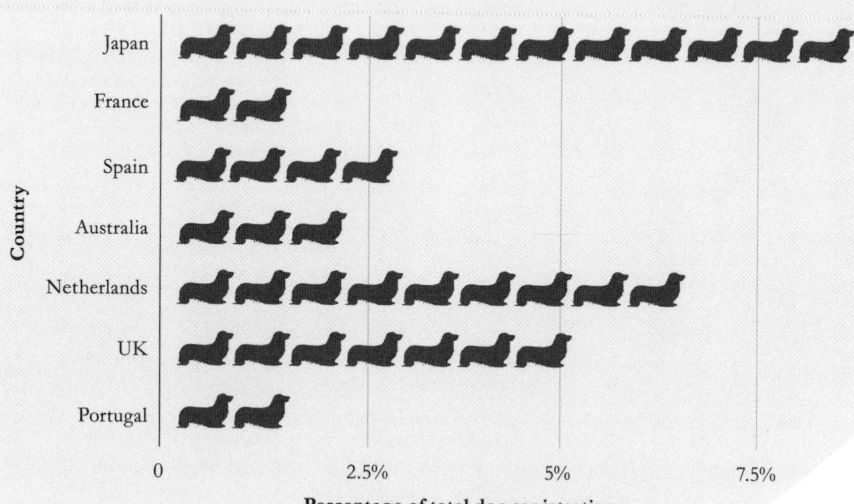

Dachshund

Of all the dogs in the Hounds group the Dachshunds stand out, or rather they don't, because they are so short. Even though the word "hound" is in their name they don't feel like Hounds, but that is how they are classified by TKC and the AKC. The FCI has them in their own distinct group.

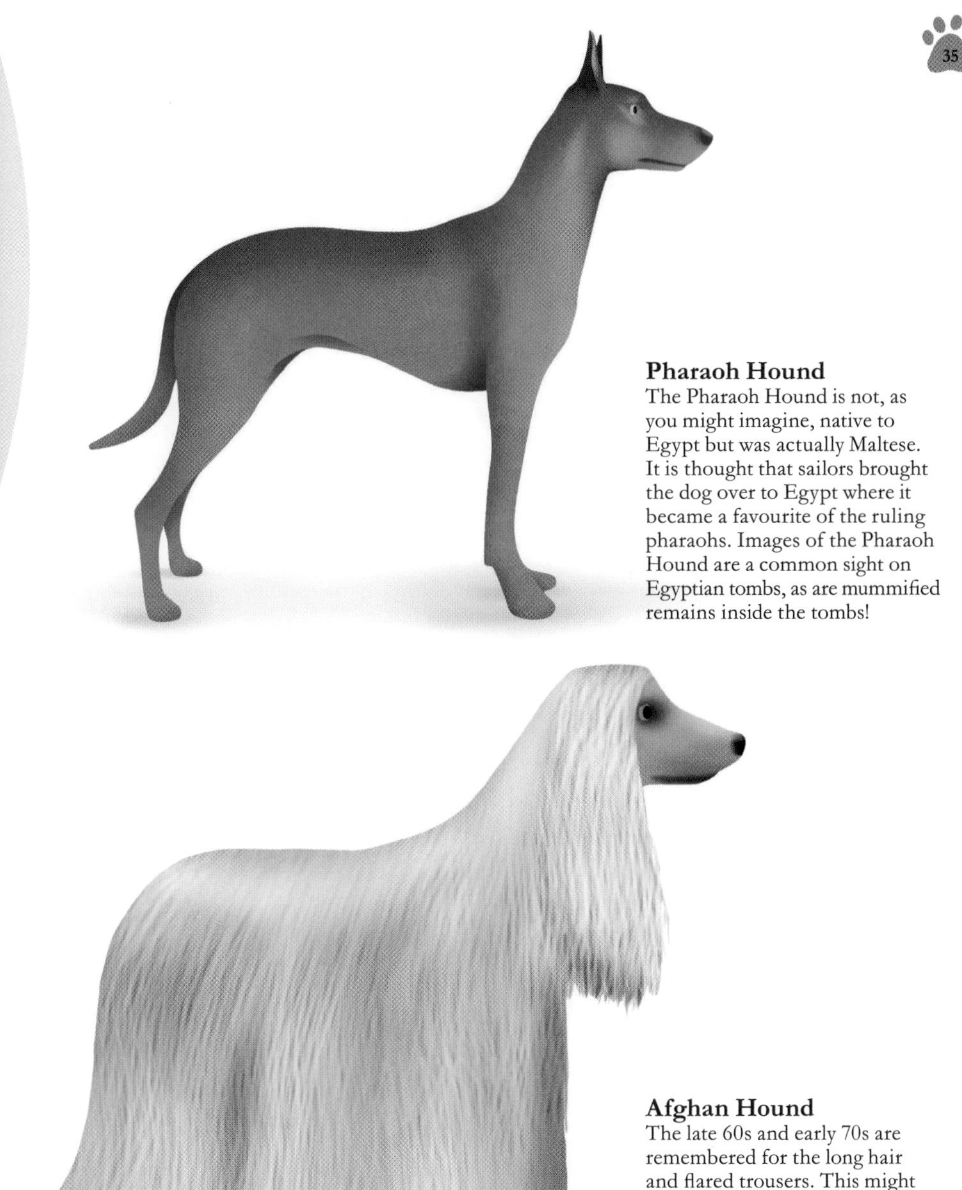

Pharaoh Hound

The Pharaoh Hound is not, as you might imagine, native to Egypt but was actually Maltese. It is thought that sailors brought the dog over to Egypt where it became a favourite of the ruling pharaohs. Images of the Pharaoh Hound are a common sight on Egyptian tombs, as are mummified remains inside the tombs!

Afghan Hound

The late 60s and early 70s are remembered for the long hair and flared trousers. This might explain why the Afghan Hound had a sudden rise in popularity which went as quickly as it had come. It could also be because in the late 1960s Barbie got herself an Afghan!

Pure Paleo Diet
Starter: meat*
Main course: meat*
Dessert: bones* and skin*
And some meat*

*Everything on the menu is BYO and is served raw.

Neolithic Mixed Diet
Hunted: wild meat
Farmed: domesticated beef, lamb, and goat
Farmed: wheat, barley, and other cereal grains

Virgil's Doggy Diner
Farmed: meat, wheat, and barley.
Roll up, roll up for a new addition to our offerings: bowls of whey!

30,000 BCE

8,000 BCE

0 CE

Gourmet for dogs

When dogs were one evolutionary step from wolves, they were carnivores eating raw meat that they had hunted and killed or scavenged. In 1980, Happidog, produced in the UK, became the first commercially available vegan dog food. What have been the steps along the way in this transformation of dogs' diets?

Diderot & D'Alembert's Deli

Today's special: Blood, liver, and heart of a slaughtered male deer combined with milk, cheese, and bread.

The Complete Farrier's Smörgåsbord

Most animal flesh and bones
Fruit
Herbs
All sorts of bread

1781 CE

1833 CE

GLOBAL CUISINE

Around the world, dogs tend to eat a pared-down version of what their owners eat. Indeed, in many parts of the world dogs still exist on the scraps from their owners' tables.

Spratt's Meat Fibrine Patent Dog Cakes

The world's first mass-produced dog biscuits, made in America.

1860 CE

Ingredients: meat, dates, and meal, combined in a biscuit form*

*No added salt

Chappel Brothers' Ken-L Ration

The first canned pet food, manufactured in the US, and made famous by Rin Tin Tin (see page 125).

1922 CE

Ingredients: horse meat, in a can

HappiDog Vegan Diet

An entirely plant-based, highly processed complete dog food, first produced and marketed in the UK.

Typical Wet Dog Food

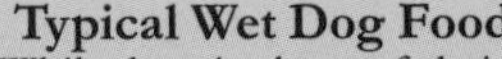

While there is plenty of choice on the dog food market today, dogs in many parts of the world eat ready-made wet food.

1980 CE

Present

Ingredients: wheat, maize, soya, wheatfeed, maize gluten meal, sugar beet pulp, sunflower oil, rice, pasta, yeast, minerals, linseed, organic rosemary, organic parsley, yucca extracts

Ingredients: water (55 per cent), meat (mainly chicken), egg, ground corn and barley, meat by-products, grits (soy), dried yeast (brewer's)

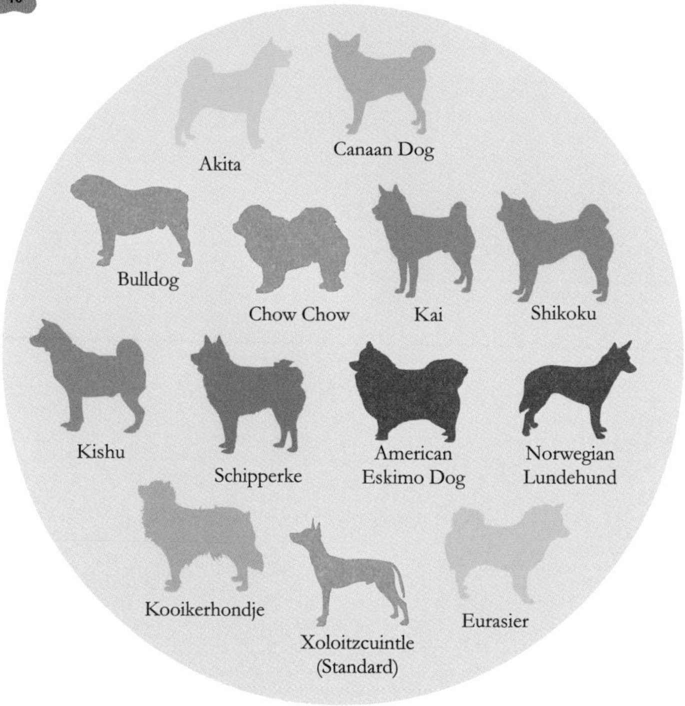

Akita
Canaan Dog
Bulldog
Chow Chow
Kai
Shikoku
Kishu
Schipperke
American Eskimo Dog
Norwegian Lundehund
Kooikerhondje
Xoloitzcuintle (Standard)
Eurasier

Shih Tzu
Poodle (Miniature and Toy)
Löwchen
Volpino

Finnish Spitz
Xoloitzcuintle (Intermediate)
Hokkaido Ainu
Shiba Inu
Akita Inu
Korean Jindo
Poodle (Standard)
Dalmatian

Schnauzer
Shar Pei
Keeshond

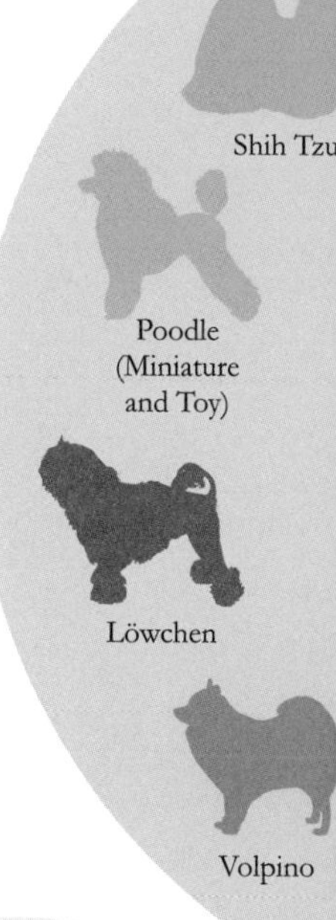

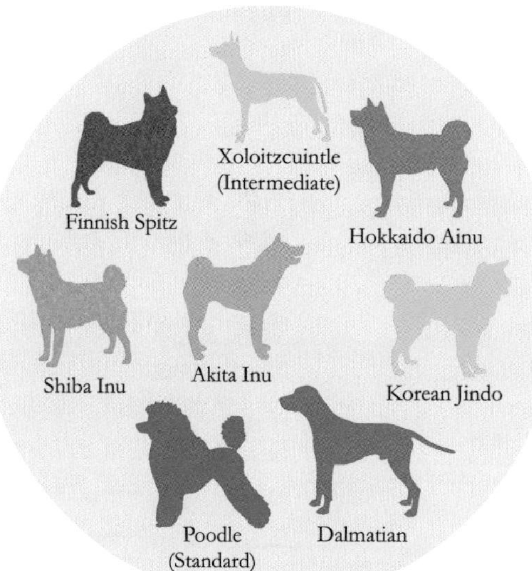

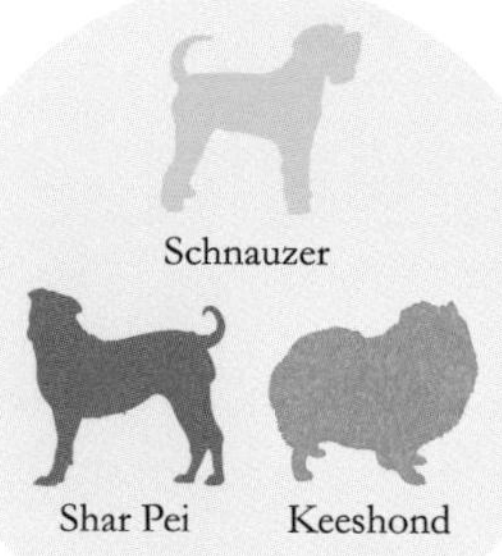

ALL SHAPES AND SIZES

Utility dogs range from diddy (Shih Tzu) to burly (Akita); from the short-haired (Xoloitzcuintle) to the hirsute (Lhasa Apso). The group could just as easily have been called Smorgasbord such is the variety.

KEY

Breed group most similar to:

- Terrier
- Working
- Gundog
- Pastoral
- Toy

Which clubs they belong to:

- The Kennel Club (TKC)
- American Kennel Club (AKC)
- Fédération Cynologique Internationale (FCI)
- TKC and AKC
- TKC and FCI
- TKC, AKC, and FCI

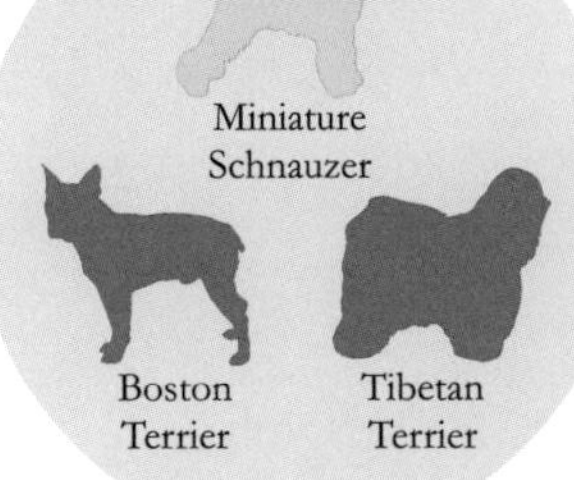

Utility dogs

These dogs are like SUVs, not that they haven't been bred for specific characteristics or tasks, it's just that they don't quite fit anywhere else. It is difficult, if not impossible, to summarize this group other than to say expect the unexpected. The AKC refers to this group simply as Non-Sporting, not to be confused with TKC's non-sporting classification.

BULLDOG POPULARITY

In the UK, the Bulldog dominated this group until the 1950s, at which point the Poodle took over before favours were equally shared out during the 1990s and 2000s. Now though the French Bulldog holds sway above all else with nearly 35 per cent of all registrations in the 2010s. The French prefer the French Bulldog and so do the Brits!

KEY

- French Bulldogs in UK
- Bulldogs in UK
- French Bulldogs in France
- Bulldogs in France

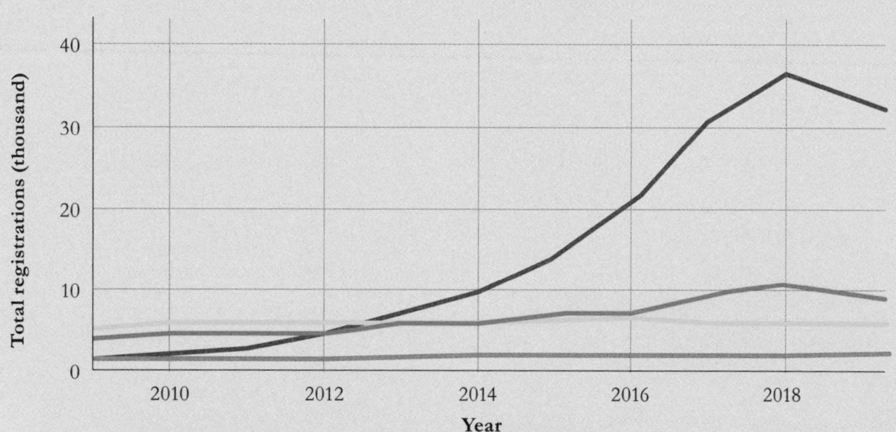

Bulldog

The Bulldog Club Incorporated is the oldest dog breed club in the world, founded in 1875. Its aim, like that of all breed clubs, is to promote the breeding of Bulldogs that are true to type. The dog itself became a symbol for British values, especially during World War II when Winston Churchill was likened to the breed.

MISCELLANY OF BREEDS

This group has some of the oldest breeds and in many cases it is their age that explains why they are in this group; the function for which they were originally bred no longer exists but they still do! Bulldogs, for example, were bred for the cruel sport of bull-baiting. In the US, this group originally also had the Toy and Working dogs before they got their own group.

French Bulldog

In recent years the French Bulldog has gone from being a reasonably popular breed to top of the pups on both sides of the Atlantic. This rise in favour can be attributed to the breed often being seen with celebrities such as Madonna, Lady Gaga, and Dwayne "The Rock" Johnson.

Xoloitzcuintle

Xoloitzcuintle may be the most difficult breed to spell and has a pronunciation that most people struggle with. This hairless dog is a native of Mexico and is known as Xolo for short. The best way to say it out loud is to split it up into bits, not the dog, the word: Sholo Eats Quint Lee.

Lost in communication

In an ideal world we speak and our dog listens, understands, and reacts perfectly to our instructions. This world does not exist but don't worry, there are things you can do to get through to your dog (see pages 56–59).

Sit
SIT!
Stay
Coming!
HEEL!
Din-dins

Don’t eat that!

There are many foods that people don’t realize are harmful to dogs, and dogs are not always able to make good decisions. While their sense of smell provides some protection, this can be tricked by foods that seem safe but have hidden dangers. It’s best to call your vet as soon as you are aware your dog has eaten something it shouldn’t, even if it doesn’t seem immediately in distress.

Chocolate

Many people don’t know this is dangerous. It is the cocoa in the chocolate that causes the problem. Dark chocolate has the most cocoa and is most likely to cause poisoning. As white chocolate has no cocoa it isn’t toxic, but it is very fatty so best to avoid.

What it does

Can cause seizures and severly increase the heart rate.

Corn on the cob

No matter how much your dog pleads with you, do not share your corn on the cob with it. Your dog’s stomach can’t digest it and it can cause serious health problems.

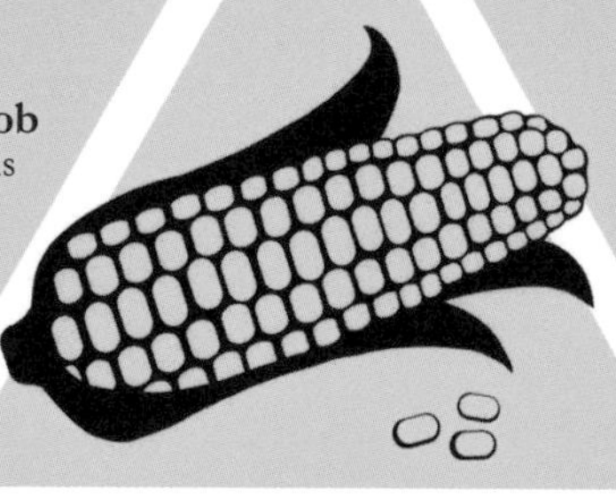

What it does

Can cause intestinal blockage.

Dairy products

Dogs are lactose-intolerant so avoid feeding them dairy products. Hard cheese, which is often used as a training treat, is low in lactose so is unlikely to cause an issue.

What it does

Can cause diarrhoea.

Furtive foraging

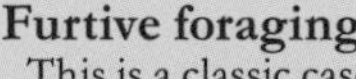

This is a classic case of dogs not thinking about consequences. They may be attracted to the food smells coming from a bin or compost heap, but the rotting food they forage could contain mycotoxins, which are very toxic to dogs.

What it does

Can cause convulsions, muscle tremors, fever, and vomiting.

Grapes or raisins

Many people think grapes, raisins, sultanas, and currants are okay for dogs. They are not. Dogs will eat them because they smell sweet, but they can have serious consequences.

What it does

Can cause kidney failure, even in very small amounts.

Garlic (also onions, leeks, and chives)

There is a belief that garlic, when added to dog food, will alleviate the need for flea treatment. The theory being that, like Dracula, fleas do not like the taste of garlic. The problem is that in larger doses garlic is dangerous for dogs.

What it does

In large amounts it can damage red blood cells, causing anaemia. It can also cause lethargy and nausea.

Medications

This should go without saying, but keep all medications out of reach of your dog. Dogs can chew a plastic bottle or blister pack open and get at the pills inside, so store them somewhere the dog can't reach. Keep your human and pet medications separate to avoid any harmful mix-ups.

What it does

Can be fatal depending on the medication. Seek expert advice from a vet.

Salted snacks

There will be a little salt in your dog's diet, but an excess can be a problem. Aside from gobbling salted snacks, the most common way a dog gets too much salt is by drinking sea water on beach walks.

What it does

Can cause vomiting and diarrhoea which lead to dehydration.

Macadamia nuts and walnuts

Nuts are very high in fat and some are salty, so not good for dogs, but some are really toxic, such as Macadamia nuts.

What it does

May cause vomiting, weakness, loss of coordination, and even depression.

Chewing gum

It's unlikely anyone would give their dog chewing gum, but the scavenging pup can easily snaffle some off the pavement. Chewing gum contains xylitol, a sugar replacement that is anything other than sweet if swallowed by a dog. It is also found in some breath mints.

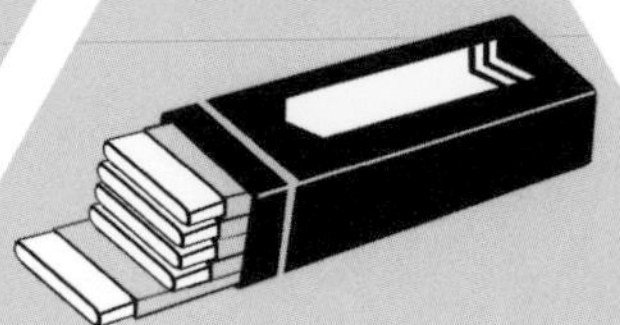

What it does

Causes hypoglycemia and liver failure.

Leftovers

Everyone knows dogs aren't just for Christmas, but that is a classic time when a pooch can hoover up scraps. Parties offer a smorgasbord for the alert dog but are packed with hidden dangers, from mince pies to chocolate and unattended alcohol dregs.

What it does

Where shall we start? Just call the vet!

Top dog

Our understanding of how dogs work within groups has changed in recent years. For a long time, it was believed that they were pack animals and needed to know their place in the pecking order to feel safe. However, as dogs' place in our lives has developed, so has our relationship with them.

Wolf pack

Wolf packs have a strict hierarchy and group dynamic, with a dominant alpha pair at the top and strict rules of conduct for survival.

- The pack has a male and a female leader.
- There is a defined pecking order.
- Position is acquired by force.
- Leaders control the pack by providing food.
- Relationships are established with play.
- A wolf may be driven out of the pack for good.
- Packs may fight each other to survive.
- Wolves don't back down if they can avoid it.
- The wolf pack avoids change.

From pack of wolves to family pet

Because dogs evolved from wolves, it was long assumed that their group dynamics were similar, with one dog dominating the pack. Early theories of dog training were based on this: you had to be top dog to make sure that your pet would know its place and do as it was told. Nowadays, the way that dogs relate to their human families is seen as more of a give and take. This is important because it affects the way we live with and train our dogs.

Family dog

When we bring a dog into our lives we are extending our family, and the dog is expected to follow the same behavioural code as other family members.

- The family has leaders, but they seek collaboration.
- There is a variable pecking order.
- Position is acquired by persuasion, humour, and labour.
- Common goals, such as food, are used to keep control.
- Relationships are established with play.
- A dog may be sent to the doghouse, but only for a while.
- Most families don't fight other families.
- A family dog may roll over.
- The family adapts to change.

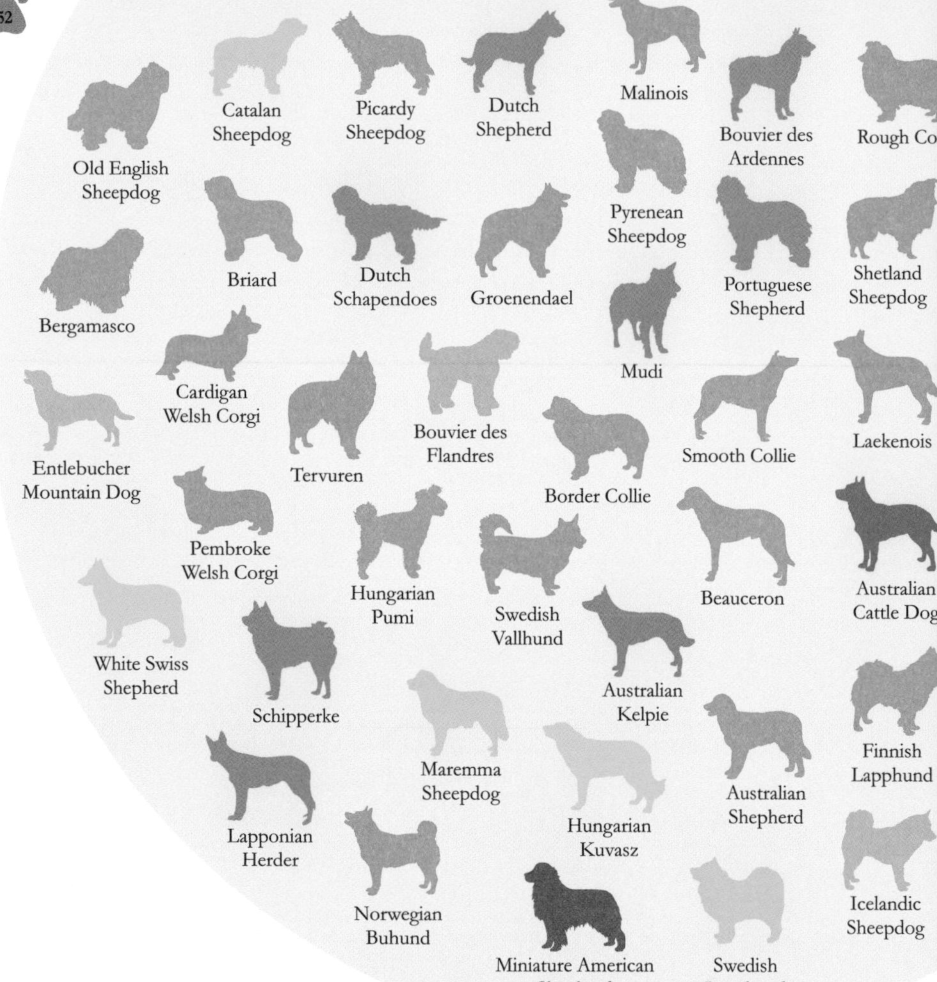

Pastoral dogs

This group belongs in the countryside and on farms doing a hard day's work corralling and protecting livestock. There are three sub-groups: herders, drovers, and guards. The AKC calls this group Herding. The FCI groups them into Group 1: Sheepdogs and Cattledogs; Group 5: Spitz and Primitive Types; and also into Group 2, which includes some cattledogs.

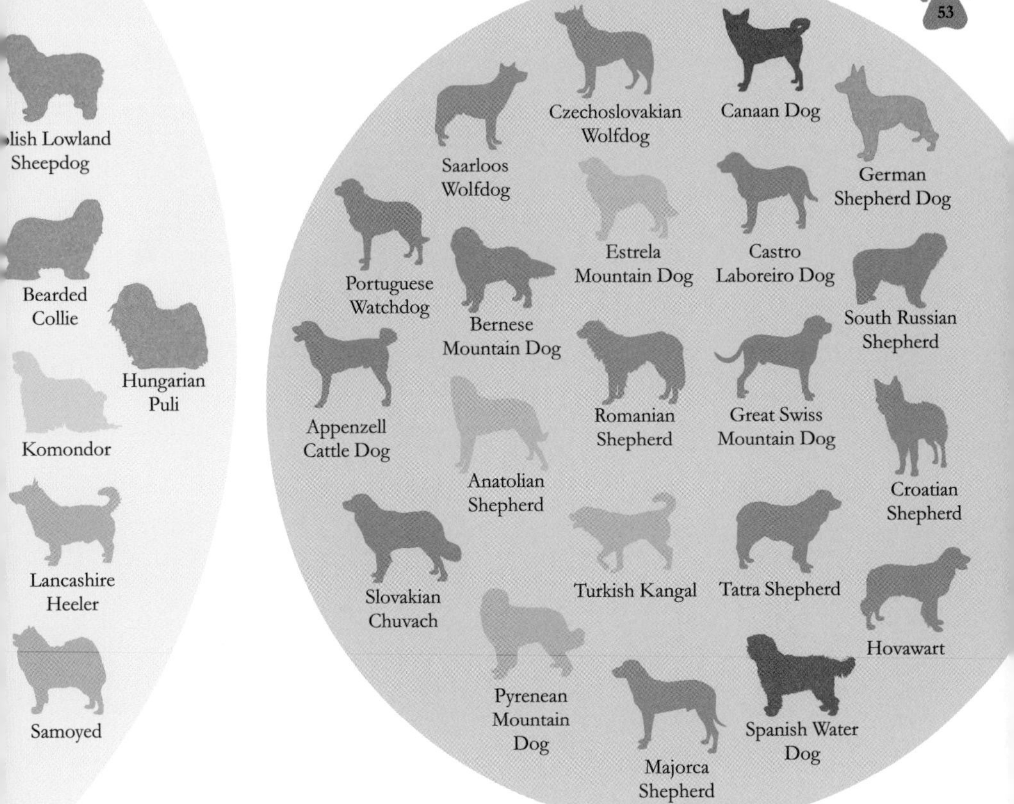

lish Lowland Sheepdog
Bearded Collie
Hungarian Puli
Komondor
Lancashire Heeler
Samoyed
Czechoslovakian Wolfdog
Canaan Dog
Saarloos Wolfdog
German Shepherd Dog
Estrela Mountain Dog
Castro Laboreiro Dog
Portuguese Watchdog
Bernese Mountain Dog
South Russian Shepherd
Appenzell Cattle Dog
Romanian Shepherd
Great Swiss Mountain Dog
Anatolian Shepherd
Croatian Shepherd
Slovakian Chuvach
Turkish Kangal
Tatra Shepherd
Hovawart
Pyrenean Mountain Dog
Majorca Shepherd
Spanish Water Dog

PASTORAL PETS

Pastoral dogs that have become pets can often be seen displaying their herding behaviour during play with humans and other dogs.

KEY

Dog type:

- Guard
- Herder/drover

Which clubs they belong to:

- The Kennel Club (TKC)
- American Kennel Club (AKC)
- Fédération Cynologique Internationale (FCI)
- TKC and AKC
- KC and FCI
- AKC and FCI
- TKC, AKC, and FCI

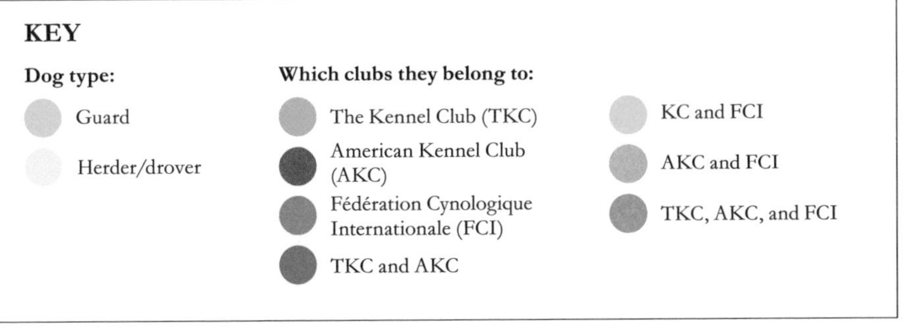

GERMAN SHEPHERD POPULARITY

During World War I, the German Shepherd was renamed Alsatian in the UK as it was felt that the use of German in the name would reduce its popularity. In 1977, after much pressure from lovers of the breed, the name was changed back to its original. In 1918, only 0.21 per cent of dogs registered in the UK were German Shepherds, but by 1926 the newly named Alsatians had hit 13.74 per cent. The breed's popularity has fluctuated in the years since.

In the US, 4.6 per cent of registered dogs are German Shepherds and two, Major and Champ Biden, currently live in the White House.

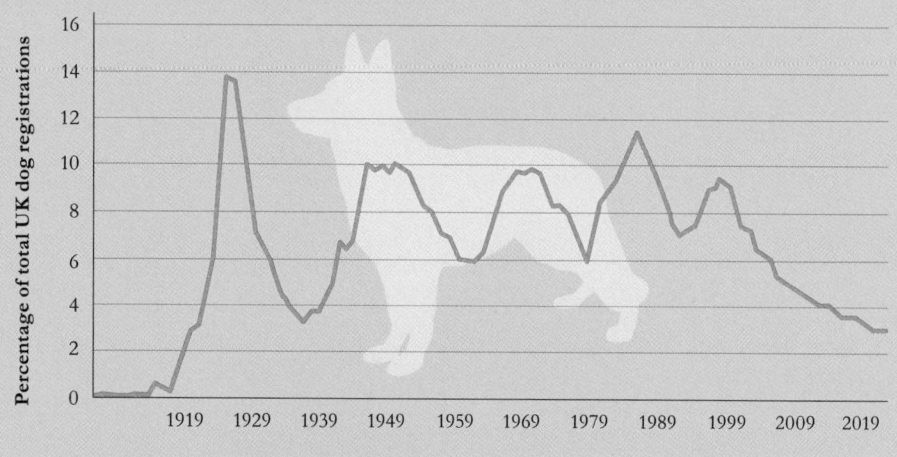

Samoyed

The Samoyed was a reindeer herder originating from the North East of Siberia. According to the TKC the breed was partly established in the UK by Antarctic Buck, a survivor of Norwegian explorer Carsten Borchgrevink's Antarctic expedition at the end of the 1800s.

Old English Sheepdog

This breed became very popular in the UK and Australia in the 1960s and 1970s thanks to being adopted as the figurehead of Dulux paint. This breed became so identified with the brand that people started referring to it simply as The Dulux Dog.

Briard

The Briard is an ancient French breed originating from the Brie-producing area of France as an all round farm dog, herding and guarding flocks. The breed was very popular in France and it was co-opted as the official war dog of the French Army during World War I.

Hear boy!

Teaching your dog to sit on command or persuading it to come back to you when it has wandered off are the first and most important parts of dog training. If you can't recall your dog, can you really let it off the lead at all? Training is built up in small steps. The key is that your dog has to want to sit or come back to you more than it wants to carry on doing what it's currently doing.

SIT AND STAY

Your dog does not know what the word sit means so you have to teach it. Repeat these stages a few times. Each time it should work more quickly as the dog understands the command and potential reward for obeying.

Step 1

With your dog standing, hold a small treat just above its nose. As it moves its mouth towards the treat, you move your hand very slightly upwards and backwards to make your dog lift its head.

Step 2

As you keep moving the treat backwards just out of reach, the tilt of your dog's head will eventually cause it to sit down.

Words and whistles

Research has shown that the actual words you use are not very important. The tone and pitch are what the dog hears and responds to; the actual word is down to your choice. The important thing is to be consistent yourself and across the whole family. Whistles and clickers are to all intents and purposes the same as words. The advantage they have is that they can be heard from further away. Make sure they are used sparingly and specifically.

Training

Any time you teach your dog something new you must do it in small increments, and while this may seem arduous, it is the only way to get the message across. Don't forget, you are speaking different languages!

The best way to teach your dog something new is when there are no distractions. Find somewhere quiet in your home or garden. Always end your training on a good note, when your dog has pleased you.

Step 3
As this is about to happen say "Sit".

Step 4
As soon as your dog sits, release the treat and give praise.

Reinforcement

Once this is working quickly go back to stage 1, but just hold the treat still and say sit. If your dog sits, reward and praise. When this progression succeeds a number of times, hold the treat further away. The final stage is being able to give the command without the treat visible.

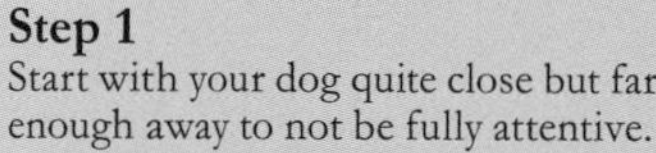

Step 1
Start with your dog quite close but far enough away to not be fully attentive.

Step 2
Attract your dog's attention by calling their name.

RECALL

Repeat the steps above to train your dog to come back to you. For subsequent training sessions, your start position should be further away from your dog. If the command doesn't work, reduce the distance between you until it does, then start to enlarge it. Between training sessions try the command out of the blue, always making sure your dog has the chance to succeed.

Rewards

You are recalling your dog because you want, or need, them to not be where they are right now. The problem is that where they are right now is somewhere they want to be. This means you have to make sure that being with you is worth more to them than being where they are, and this is where the rewards comes in.

The reward has to be of value to them and this varies from dog to dog. The three main rewards are food, toys, and praise. You will quickly discover which of these is most valuable to your dog and you can then use it wisely to train your dog to come back to you.

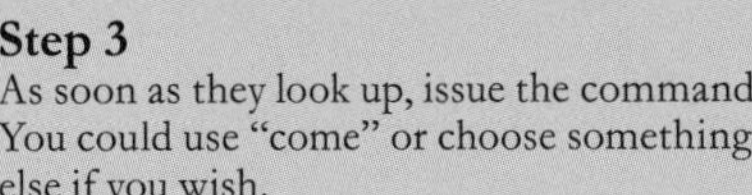

Step 3
As soon as they look up, issue the command. You could use "come" or choose something else if you wish.

Step 4
Just say the command once, allowing your dog the chance to succeed.

Step 5
As soon as they make a small move towards you, reward them.

Distractions
When you are getting success in quiet conditions at home start to introduce some distractions and build up to practising it out in public. If you're concerned, try it first with a long lead, allowing slack.

Who's in charge?

The best-trained dog's only control device is their master's voice; for the rest there are other options. The connection between dog and master is the lead and collar. Choosing the right combination is essential for good teamwork.

COLLARS

The lead must be attached to your dog, but how? Consider where on the animal – head, neck, or shoulders – is best for your dog and how you want to control it. Then you can think about style choices.

Martingale collar
This collar provides control without the cruel choking effect of a choke collar, because its design limits the amount of tightening. Used properly, it can be an effective training tool.

Choke collar
As the name suggests, this has a choking action. The collar is loose and is tightened by pulling on the lead. It is cruel and can cause injury if used incorrectly – avoid.

LEADS

These come in a variety of materials, styles, and lengths. It may take a while to find what works best for you and your dog.

Long lead
Up to 30 m (100 ft) long, this is good for training if you are unsure of your dog's recall. It gives the dog a little freedom, and you a safety net.

Standard lead
Around 2 m (6 ft) long, this is used mainly for walking by roads, or in parks and open spaces where dogs must be kept on a lead.

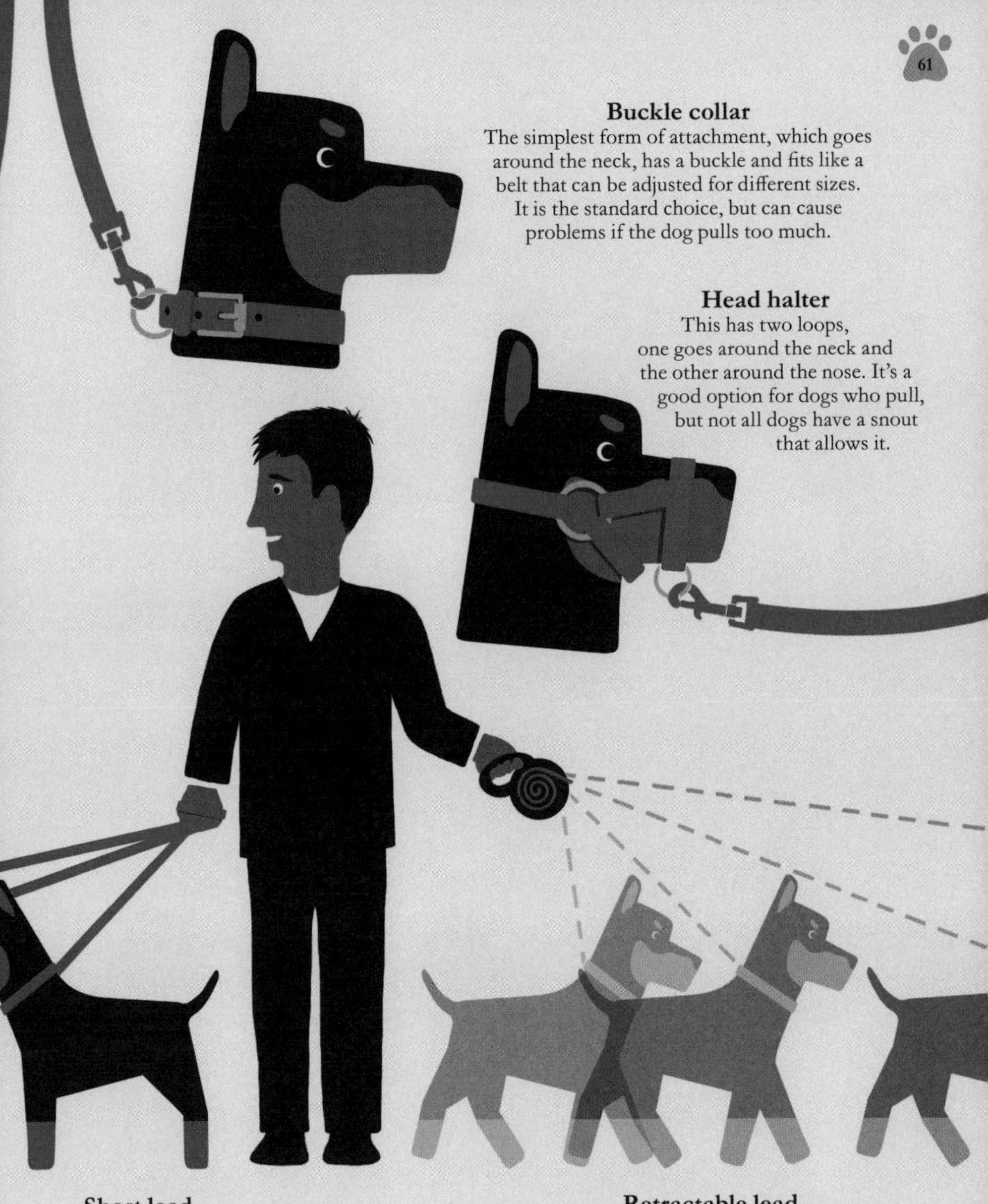

Buckle collar

The simplest form of attachment, which goes around the neck, has a buckle and fits like a belt that can be adjusted for different sizes. It is the standard choice, but can cause problems if the dog pulls too much.

Head halter

This has two loops, one goes around the neck and the other around the nose. It's a good option for dogs who pull, but not all dogs have a snout that allows it.

Short lead

Between 25 cm (10 in) and 1 m (3 ft) long, this is useful when you need to keep your dog close and helps to stop the dog pulling.

Retractable lead

This is a more easily adjustable version of the long lead. There is debate about its value as you have less control and wire versions can be dangerous.

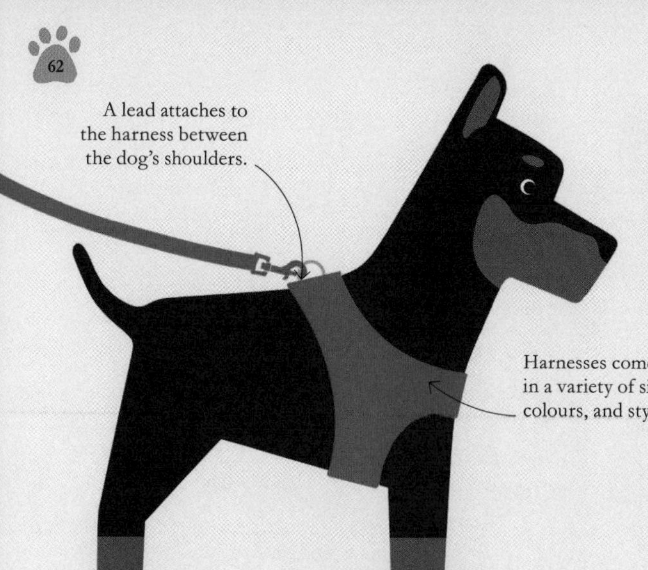

Harness

This is secured around the dog's shoulders and chest, so it has nothing around its neck. The lead is usually attached at the back. It is especially good for large or strong dogs that pull, to avoid neck pressure, or for tiny dogs with delicate necks.

Muzzles

There are two main reasons for a muzzle. The first is to prevent dogs who can't stop themselves from eating things they find – not always limited to food! The second is for dogs whose owners can't control their dogs' tempers. Outbursts may be sparked by specific things or certain other breeds and the muzzle stops the dog doing something its owner will regret.

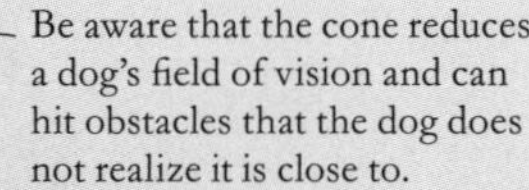
Be aware that the cone reduces a dog's field of vision and can hit obstacles that the dog does not realize it is close to.

Cone

Possibly the saddest sight is that of a dog in a cone. This usually means they have had an operation or received an injury. The cone is to stop them getting to the wound and licking or nibbling it. Cones are also used when something has been applied to the skin, such as an antiseptic cream – the cone will stop the dog licking the cream off.

Controlling your dog

It is always the dog owner's responsibility to restrain the dog and make sure it does not bother other people.

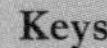

Keys
You should take your dog to the vet as soon as you suspect it has swallowed something that is unlikely to pass through naturally.

Balls
Some dogs just don't seem to know that balls are for playing with and not to be swallowed.

Inside out

There was story in the papers at the end of 2019 about a young Spaniel. It kept eating things it shouldn't. These included tennis balls, tights, and even its own toys. A leather muzzle was fitted on the dog to try to stop this habit. The dog ate it.

Cutlery
Scoffing a plateful of food before being caught can lead to forks, spoons, and even knives being ingested too.

Fish hooks
The problem here is the bait or the fish. It is these that the dog may try to eat, not realizing a hook is present.

Sticks
There are many reasons why a dog may eat a stick. These include boredom, hunger, nutritional deficiencies, and tooth problems.

Socks
In 2014, a Great Dane in Portland, Oregon, USA, had 43½ socks removed from it during emergency abdominal surgery.

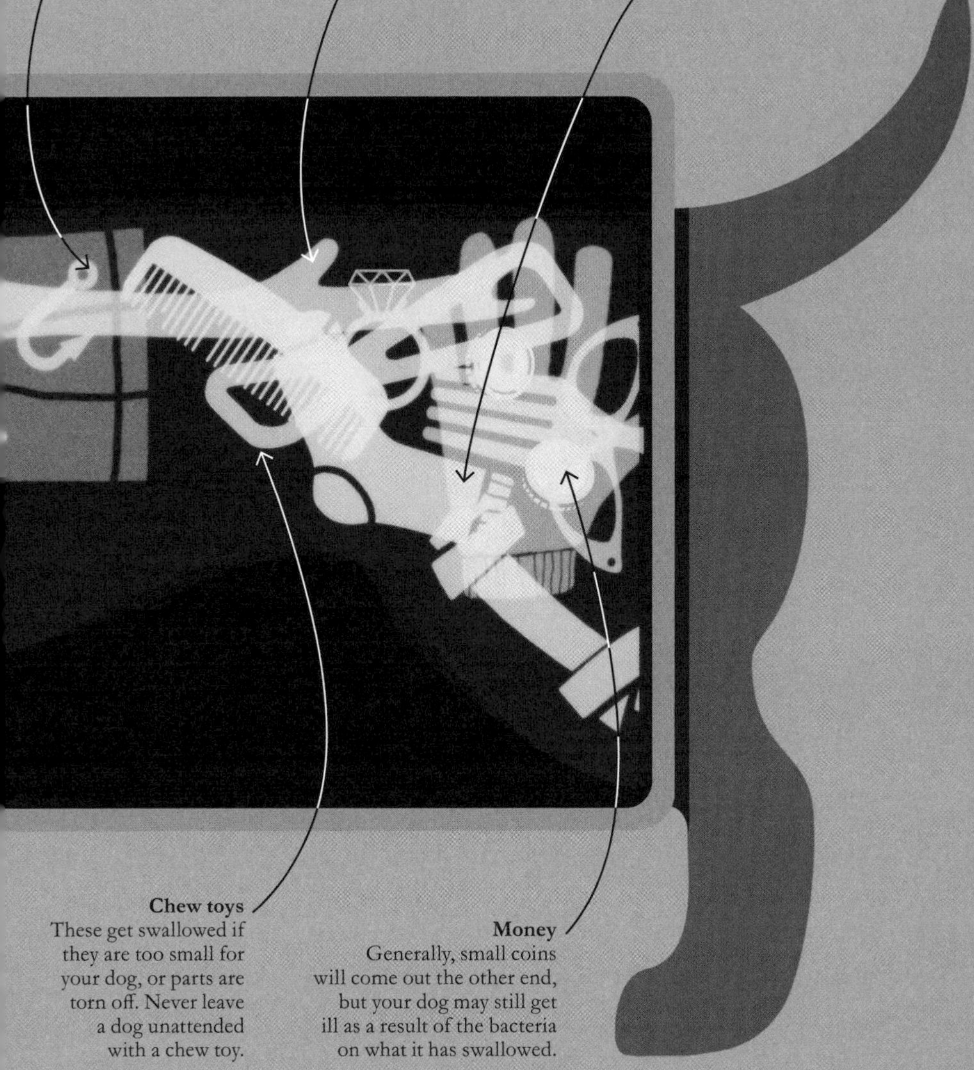

Chew toys
These get swallowed if they are too small for your dog, or parts are torn off. Never leave a dog unattended with a chew toy.

Money
Generally, small coins will come out the other end, but your dog may still get ill as a result of the bacteria on what it has swallowed.

Dogs in literature

A lot of people think super-sleuth Sherlock Holmes was a real person. The legendary investigator is probably more famous than any detective who actually lived – and the same is true of many fictional dogs. Holmes himself comes across one of literature's most infamous canines in the third novel about the detective by British writer Arthur Conan Doyle. The eponymous anti-hero of that story is a good place to start. *Warning: the following pages may contain spoilers!*

KEY
The author has awarded each dog a star rating out of five for its literary stature, based on a range of criteria.

Fame How well-known the dog is

Plot Points The importance of the dog to the storyline

Adaptations Comparing how often a dog appears in other media

Sequels The number of books involving the same dog

Charisma The dog's star quality

Bloodhound-Mastiff cross

THE HOUND OF THE BASKERVILLES

Set on Dartmoor, a boggy upland in Devon, England, *The Hound of the Baskervilles* follows Sherlock Holmes' attempt to solve the murder of Sir Charles Baskerville. He appears to have been killed by the mythical baying beast of the title. Holmes and his sidekick, Dr Watson, discover that the hound is no myth but a real dog owned by the killer, who meets his end in the deadly Grimpen Mire.

Fame	★★★★★
Plot Points	★★★★★
Adaptations	★★★★★
Sequels	☆☆☆☆☆
Charisma	★★★★☆

ARGOS

Homer's *Odyssey* tells the story of ancient Greek hero Odysseus' long journey home after the Trojan War. While Argos appears only in the 17th of the epic poem's 22 books, his role is vital. Odysseus has been away so long that no one recognizes him. It is not until Argos lies down and dies on seeing his master that the hero's identity is proven.

Fame	★★★☆☆
Plot Points	★★★★★
Adaptations	★★★☆☆
Sequels	☆☆☆☆☆
Charisma	★★★☆☆

RENNI

The hero of *Renni the Rescuer: A Dog of the Battlefield* is a military dog in a fictitious war in a fictitious country in Europe. The book's Austrian author, Felix Salten, is best known for his earlier novel, *Bambi*. First published in 1940, Renni's tale covers his life from puppy through to being wounded during duty as a rescue dog in the war.

Fame	★★★☆☆
Plot Points	★★★★★
Adaptations	☆☆☆☆☆
Sequels	☆☆☆☆☆
Charisma	★★★★☆

CRAB

English playwright William Shakespeare wrote many memorable lines about dogs, such as the "dog will have his day" in *Hamlet*, but he only gave a name to one canine character – in *The Two Gentlemen of Verona*. Crab is the companion of Launce, a servant to one of the gentlemen. The pair provide the play's funniest moments thanks to Launce's soliloquies and Crab's reactions to them.

Breed unknown

Fame	★★★☆☆
Plot Points	★★★☆☆
Adaptations	☆☆☆☆☆
Sequels	☆☆☆☆☆
Charisma	★★★☆☆

ERLANG SHEN'S DOG

Mythological Chinese god Erlang Shen appears in several novels accompanied by his unnamed dog, who is always on hand to help his master. They first appear in *Journey to the West* by Ming dynasty author Wu Cheng'en. In this novel, the dog's most significant intervention is biting Sun Wukong, the Monkey King, on the leg during a climactic fight.

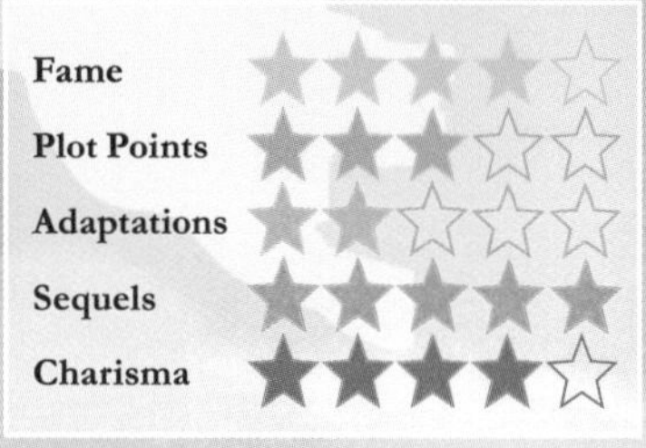

Fame	★★★★☆
Plot Points	★★★☆☆
Adaptations	★★☆☆☆
Sequels	★★★★★
Charisma	★★★★☆

SCRAGGLY

First published in Korean in 2012 and in English in 2016, *The Dog Who Dared to Dream* has sold more than two million copies. It tells the story of a dog who is an outsider but dreams of a better life. She and her master have a tough life, but through companionship and courage they get through hard times together and find happiness.

Fame	★★★☆☆
Plot Points	★★★★★
Adaptations	☆☆☆☆☆
Sequels	☆☆☆☆☆
Charisma	★★★★☆

TOP OF THE PUPS

These literary dog stars have been judged on an assortment of qualities. Some, such as how often their tales have been adapted for screen or stage, can be measured objectively, while others, such as fame or charisma, are based on the author's whim. Feel free to disagree. Here are our overall winners and losers.

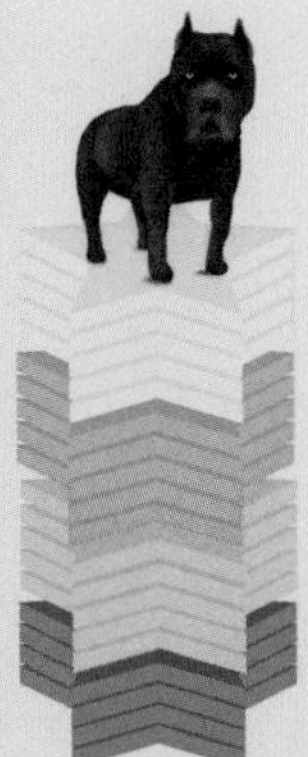

Hound of the Baskervilles

Argos

Renni

Crab

Erlang Shen's dog

Scraggly

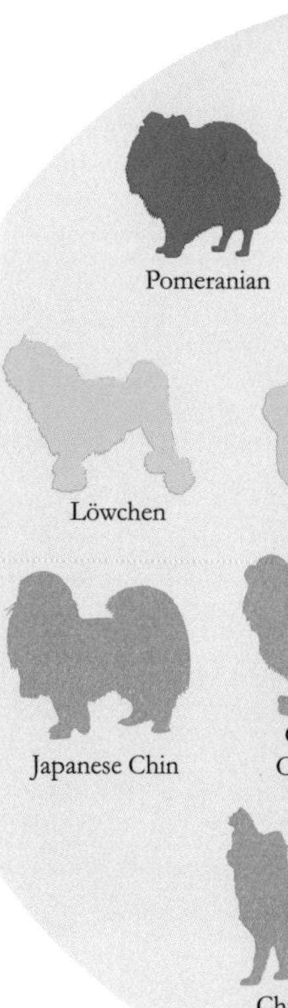

Pomeranian

Papillon

Pekingese

Standard Poodle

Löwchen

Bolognese

Pug

Bichon Frise

Japanese Chin

Cavalier King Charles Spaniel

King Charles Spaniel

Maltese

Boston Terrier

Chihuahua (Long-haired)

Chihuahua (Short-haired)

Miniature Pinscher

Coton de Tulear

Tibetan Spaniel

Manchester Terrier (Toy)

English Toy Terrier

Miniature Poodle

Russian Toy

Yorkshire Terrier

Italian Greyhound

French Bulldog

Toy Poodle

Miniature Schnauzer

Toy Fox Terrier

STAND-ALONE BREED

The Standard Poodle is the odd-one out here. The AKC and TKC put this breed in the Non-Sporting/Utility group, but for the FCI it's a toy!

KEY

Dog types:

- Traditional lapdogs
- Bred smaller from another breed
- Small dog
- Other

Which clubs they belong to:

- The Kennel Club (TKC)
- American Kennel Club (AKC)
- Fédération Cynologique Internationale (FCI)
- TKC and AKC
- TKC and FCI
- AKC and FCI
- TKC, AKC, and FCI

Toy dogs

The FCI refers to this group as Companion dogs and this is a good way to think of them. They are the only group that was not bred as working dogs, but that should not make us think any less of them. Being a companion is a 24-hour job and this group lives up to its name perfectly.

Russian Toy

The Russian Toy may only stand at around 25 cm (10 in) tall but it is a hardy little breed that survived the Russian Revolution. With its links to the aristocracy it could easily have been wiped out when the monarchy was abolished. It was only recognized by TKC in 2017.

SMALL DOGS, BIG PERSONALITIES

The title "Toy" also refers to their diminutive size; they are all, without exception, small, but only in stature – they are packed with personality beyond their physical scale.

The group is a mixture of traditional lapdogs and versions of the other groups that have been bred down to a smaller size. It's worth noting that not all Toys are lapdogs, and not all lapdogs are Toys! This group includes some of the earliest recognized breeds.

Most popular

There appears to be little consensus about which Toy is the best. These are the most popular Toy breeds in each country and how they rank compared to all breeds.

Brazil
Pomeranian

UK
Pug

Holland
French Bulldog

South Africa
Pomeranian

USA
Yorkshire Terrier

Australia
Cavalier King Charles Spaniel

Japan
Chihuahua

Portugal
French Bulldog

South Korea
Bichon Frise

France
Cavalier King Charles Spaniel

Pug

Almost a third of all Toys registered in the UK in the 2010s were Pugs. In fact, more were registered during that decade than in the 100 years previously! This has been driven by a lot of celebrities owning them as well as there being some huge internet stars such as Doug the Pug, who has nearly 15 million followers across the various platforms.

King Charles Cavalier

There is a statue of Nell Gwyn, the mistress of King Charles II, above the entrance to a block of flats on Sloane Avenue, London, which bear her name. At her feet is a King Charles Cavalier Spaniel, a breed named after her amour.

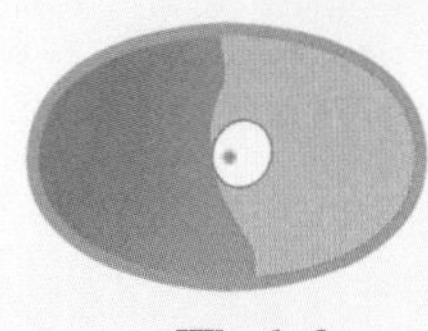

Week 3
The blastocyst implants into the wall of the uterus, which will supply nutrients and life support. Now an embryo, it is less than 1 cm (0.4 inch) long.

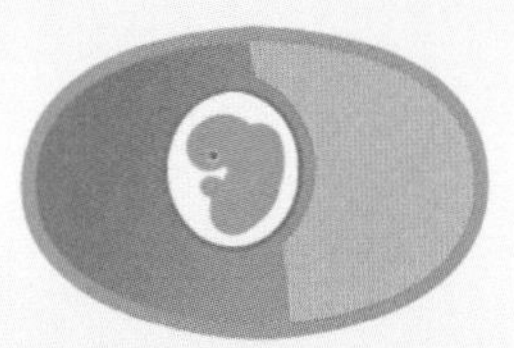

Week 4
By now, the head and eyes will have developed. At this time the mother's behaviour may change to show she is pregnant, although this won't be visible in her shape.

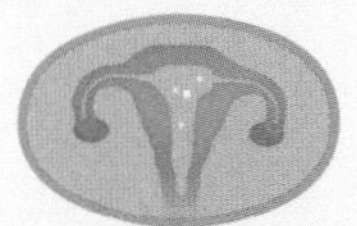

Week 2
As the fertilized cells move into the uturus they divide and form a berry-like structure called a blastocyst.

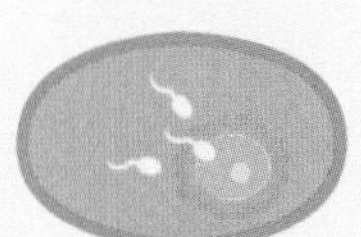

Week 1
Fertilization of one or more eggs takes place and the clock starts ticking.

No make-up is worn during pregnancy.

Gestation

Pregnancy in dogs lasts around 63 days, or just over two months. By comparison, this is less than a quarter of the gestation time for humans, but three times that for the average mouse. The period of a dog's development in utero is a similar length to that of cats and wolves, but longer than that of foxes.

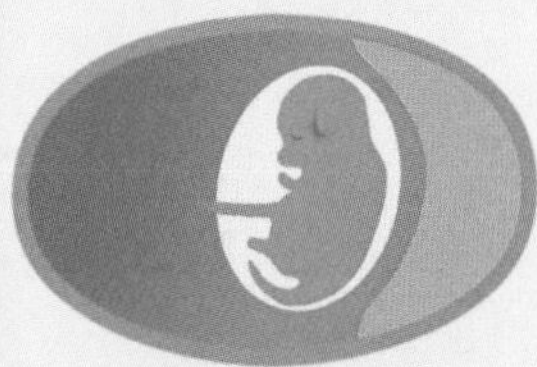

Week 5
Organs have formed and sex is set. The fetus will almost double in size this week and look like a puppy with legs, toes, and a tail.

Week 6
This is when the puppy enters the final stages of development. Claws will appear.

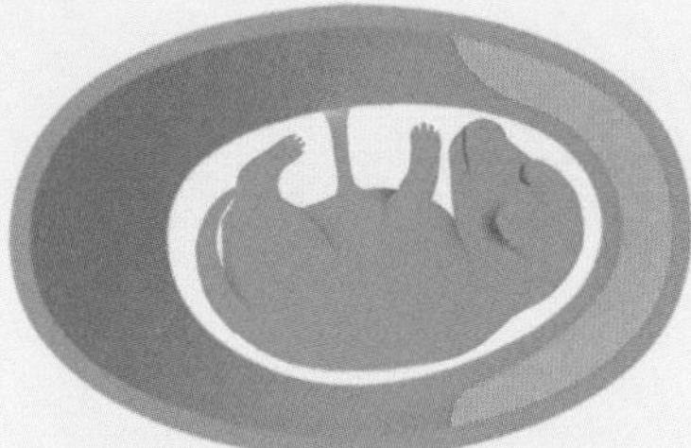

Week 7
The bones will have calcified sufficiently to show up on X-rays. The mother will be visibly pregnant and her nipples will be pink and surround by a hairless patch.

The average dog litter size is five or six. It's possible for a litter to have several fathers.

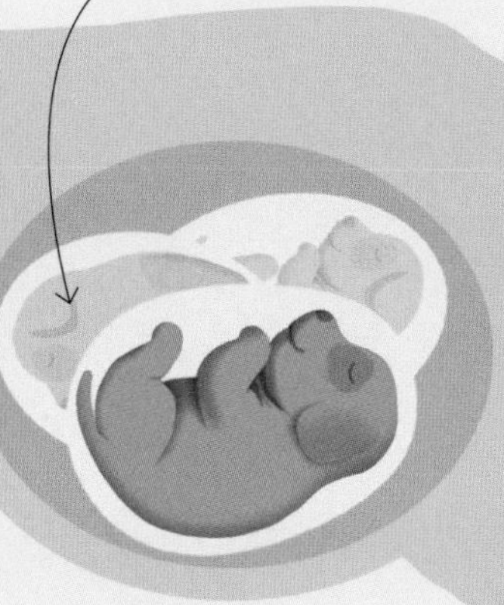

Week 9
The mother will start looking for a calm area to begin nesting. She may seem apprehensive and fractious.

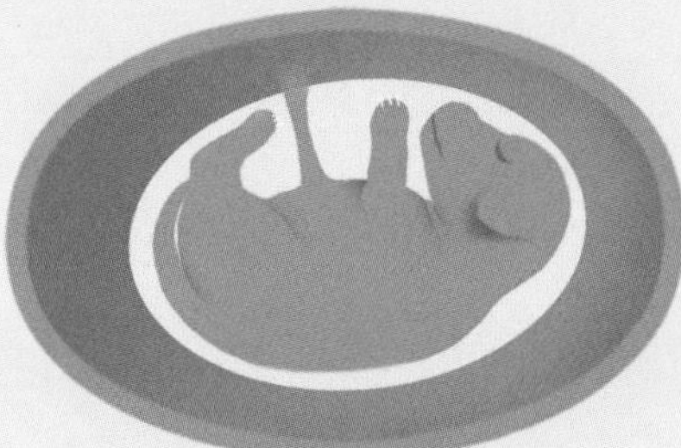

Week 8
The puppy is covered in fur now and ready to be born, but usually comes around the ninth week.

Newborn

When a puppy is born it is incredibly cute, but it won't know this because it can't see. It also can't hear and it has no teeth. It can't walk and is totally helpless, and so is reliant on its mother.

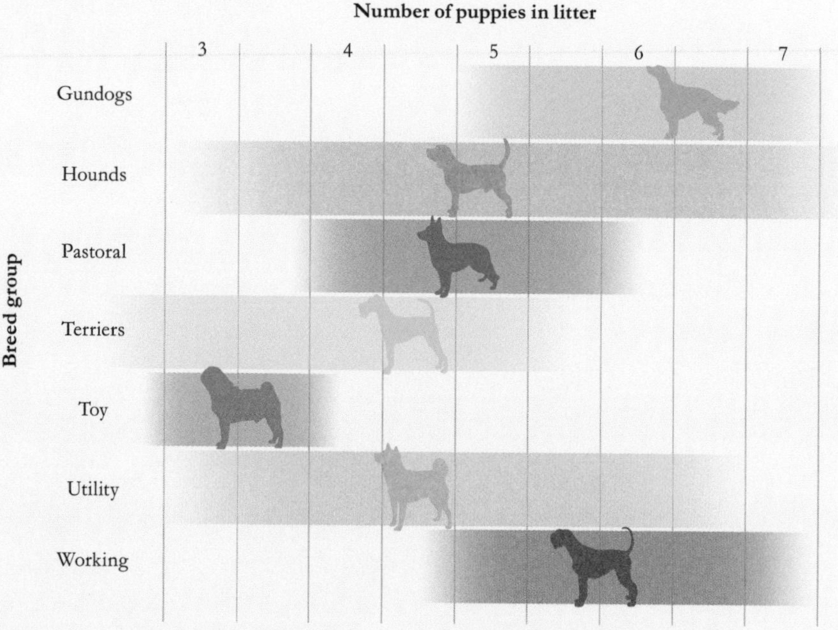
Number of puppies in litter
3
4
5
6
7
Breed group
Gundogs
Hounds
Pastoral
Terriers
Toy
Utility
Working

LITTER SIZE IN DIFFERENT BREED GROUPS

This graph shows the mean litter sizes for the different breed groups, and range around that mean. In general, the bigger the breed, the larger the litter size.

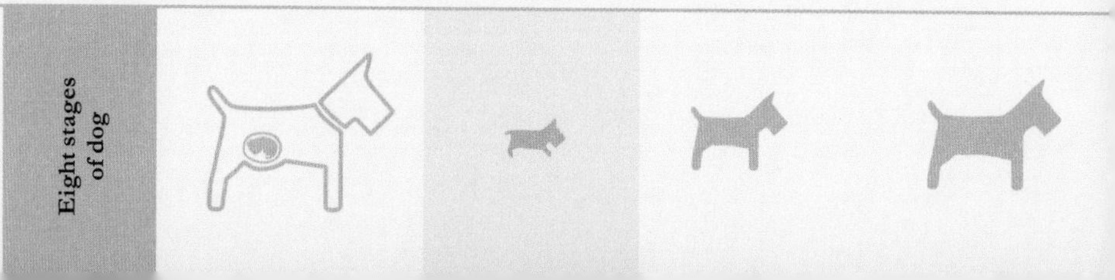
Eight stages of dog

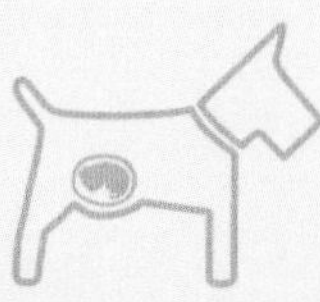

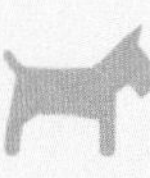

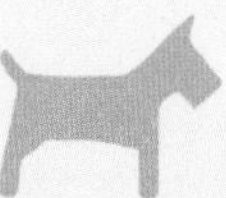

HELPLESS PUP

The first couple of weeks are filled with four things: keeping warm, eating, sleeping, and grooming. All of these are reliant on the mum's presence. In spite of its lack of facilities, a newborn pup can instinctively find its mother's nipple to begin feeding.

Walking and tail wagging
The puppy will interact with its siblings and start walking. Its tail will wag and it will be able to give out squeaky barks.

Grooming
As well as keeping them clean, grooming by the mother also involves stimulating the puppy's need to wee and poo by licking the necessary parts.

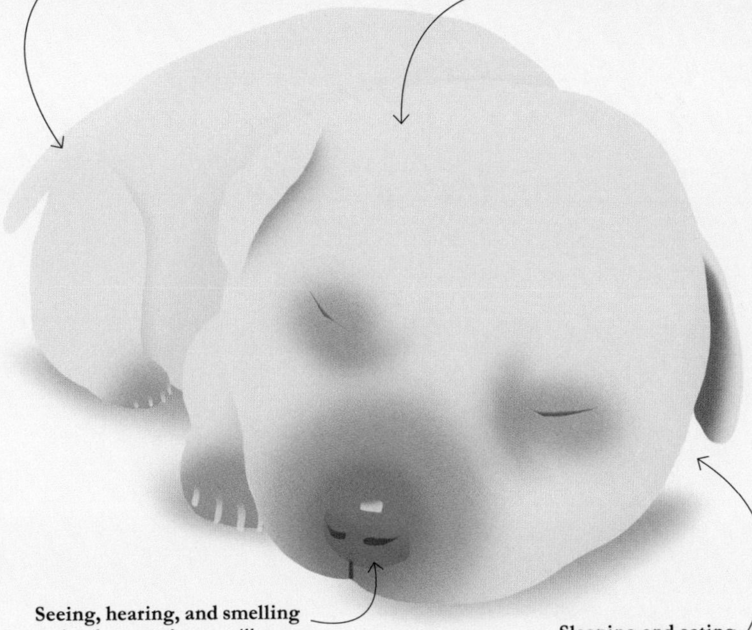

Seeing, hearing, and smelling
By two weeks, the puppy's eyes will open and it will start to become aware of a world beyond its mother. Its senses of smell and hearing develop, and baby teeth appear (28 of them) between three to six weeks.

Sleeping and eating
The newborn will sleep for up to 22 hours a day, waking every now and then to feed. At this stage it can only manage a slow crawl.

Puppy

Now that the puppy can walk, bark, and has teeth, the fun really starts. As the puppy grows it has a lot of energy, in bursts, but is not yet allowed out. For the moment its world is its siblings and the early learning begins.

Solid food (3–4 weeks)

A puppy eats its first solid food at around three weeks. Toilet training starts then too. Dogs are instinctively tidy animals and will be inclined to clear up the poop themselves unless stopped from doing so.

Play (4 weeks)

There will be lots of play fighting, biting, and yelping as the litter establishes a temporary and ever-changing hierarchy. These games help the puppy to start working out its physicality: how to lie down, stand up, jump, and roll about.

Vaccinations (8–18 weeks)

Which vaccinations a puppy needs and at what date varies from country to country, and in some places they are a legal requirement. Vaccinations come in two or three batches and will then be boosted on an annual basis. These are important to enable the puppy to mix safely with other dogs and animals.

Walks (from 12 weeks)

With vaccines on board, the puppy will be allowed out and about for walks. Puppies tire quickly, so short, frequent exercise and play opportunities are best for healthy development.

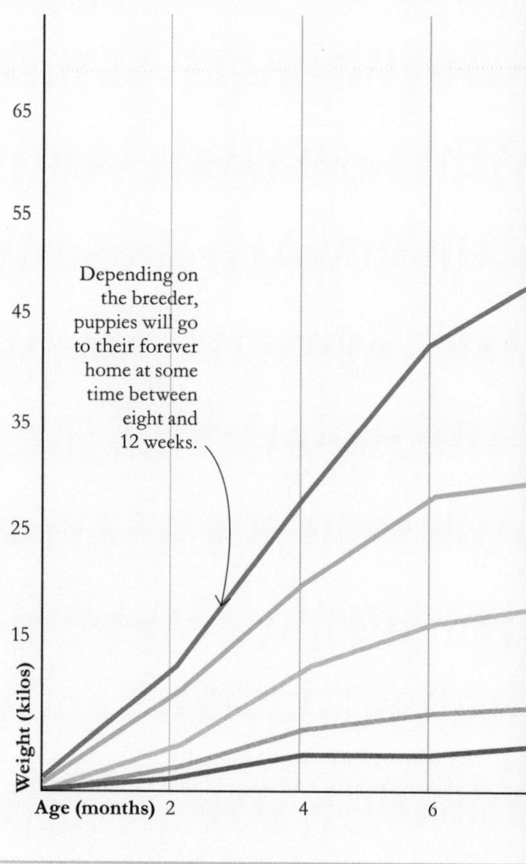

PUPPY GROWTH

While all newborns are tiny, miniature breeds reach full size within a year, but giant breeds just keep on growing. It is important not to over-feed a growing dog as excessive weight gain can cause joint problems in its developing musculoskeletal system.

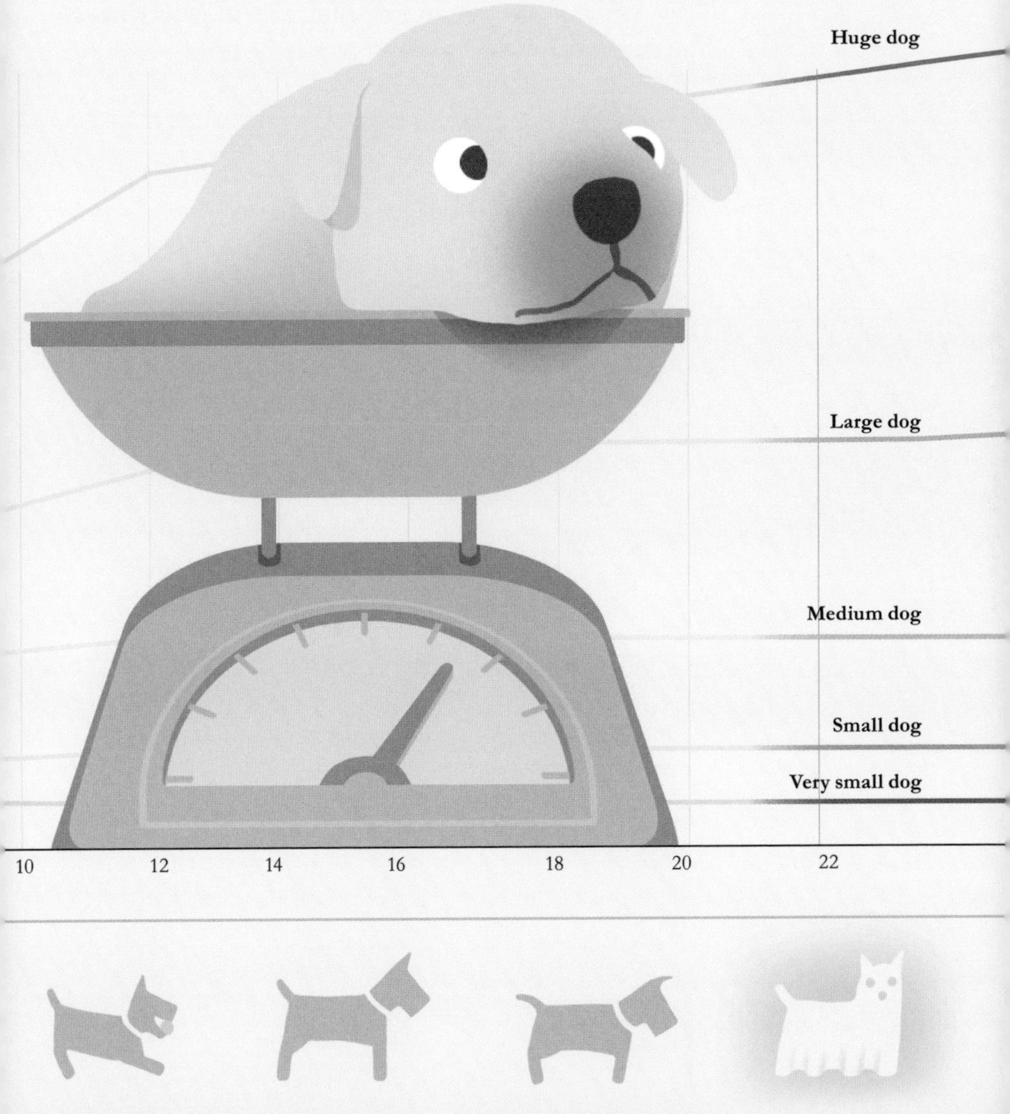

Huge dog

Large dog

Medium dog

Small dog

Very small dog

10 12 14 16 18 20 22

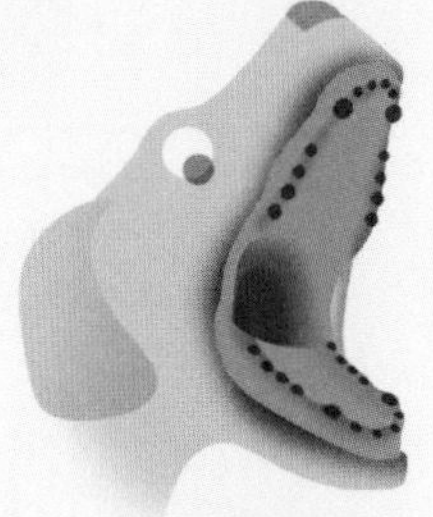

Youngster

As the early puppy stage ends, baby teeth are replaced with adult teeth. This signals the arrival of chewing. It is good practice to start brushing the dog's teeth as the adult teeth appear, to keep them in healthy condition and help avoid gum disease.

Baby teeth
No one knows where they go. Don't worry about it.

Socialization

Now that the puppy can go for walks, its horizons are expanding. Its sense of smell is strong but it doesn't know what all these smells mean. Combine this curiosity with the adult teeth pushing through and the result is that everything within reach may well get chewed to destruction.

The youngster will have had all its jabs by now and the process of socialization will have started. Being able to go out and about and mix with other dogs is an exciting time and another step in the dog's learning process. Play fighting with siblings, who are all the same age and similar size, is one thing, but it's totally different to match up with dogs of all ages, sizes, and temperaments. Socialization classes can help with this.

Signs that a play fight might be tipping over the edge:

- Hackles rising
- Low growl – which is very different to louder play-growling
- Movement is more deliberate, less energetic.
- Tucked tails

Chewing a slipper

Dogs can't spit, but you can teach them to drop. This is a good idea to stop things being chewed to destruction.

Chewing arms

Don't let this happen. Offer just the straight back of your hand so it can be licked but not bitten.

Chewing furniture

The only method for discovering what a smell means is to grab it with its mouth and give it a chew.

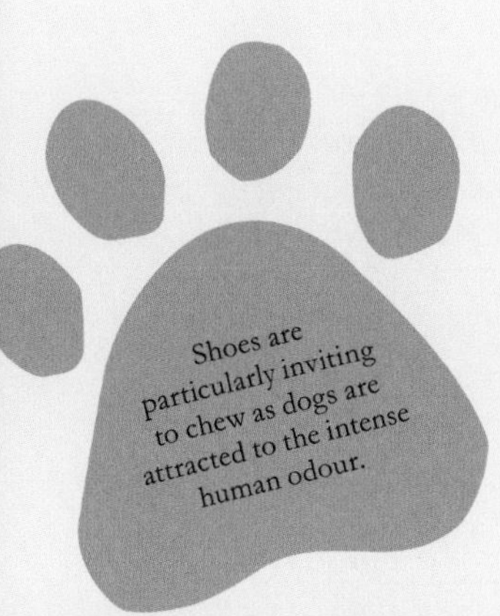

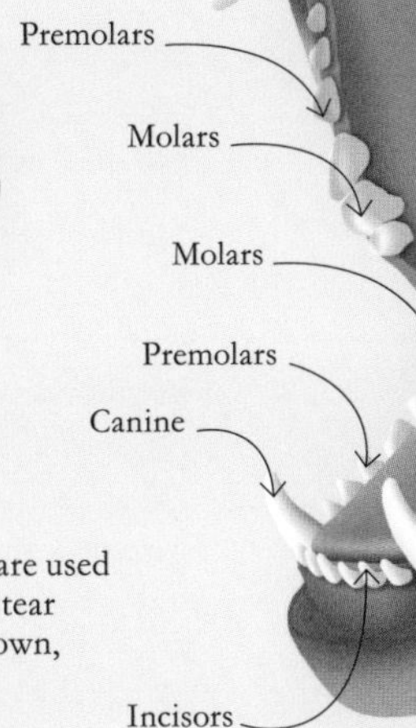

Adult teeth

An adult dog has 42 teeth. Incisors are used to scrape meat from bones, canines tear food apart, premolars break food down, and molars are used for chewing.

Adolescence

Dogs reach full size and maturity at some point between 6–18 months, depending on breed, so this period of up to a year covers what equates to the teenage years. There are many similarities to human teenagers as the dog grows quicker than its emotions and its ability to control its body.

Teenage rebellion

Almost regardless of breed, the dog will have huge amounts of energy; exercise is important to allow muscles to grow to match the bones. Training is tested as the dog pushes the limits of what is allowed, like a human teenager rebelling. Because of this it is during this period that a dog is most likely to be returned to the breeder or given to a rescue home. Over 90 per cent of such dogs have not had obedience training.

Where allowed, dogs will generally be walking off lead and so it is important that the recall command is well established. There's a fine line between a dog exploring the world and a dog getting lost.

Sexual maturity

This is also when dogs reach sexual maturity. For the owners of bitches it is important to have an understanding of the oestrus cycle. Owners of males will be faced with situations where their dog suddenly races off towards a distant, possibly unseen, bitch.

Neutering

It is not surprising then that owners will consider neutering their dog. In the female it means no unwanted bleeding on the carpet, harassment from male dogs, or unwanted pups. In the male it generally makes them less aggressive, more laid back in temperament, and less likely to stray

KEY

Proestrus: Non-fertile
Lasts about 9 days, bitch will reject advances, bleeding starts

Oestrus: Fertile
Lasts 3–11 days, bitch will accept advances

Diestrus: Non-fertile
Lasts up to 2 months

Anestrus: Non-fertile
Lasts between 5 and 7 months

Ovulation

Day 0

Luteinizing hormone

OESTRUS CYCLE IN FEMALE DOGS

A bitch will come into heat approximately twice a year, but when it happens she becomes a target for attention from most male dogs. This can make going for walks quite difficult and some owners will avoid going to public places during this time.

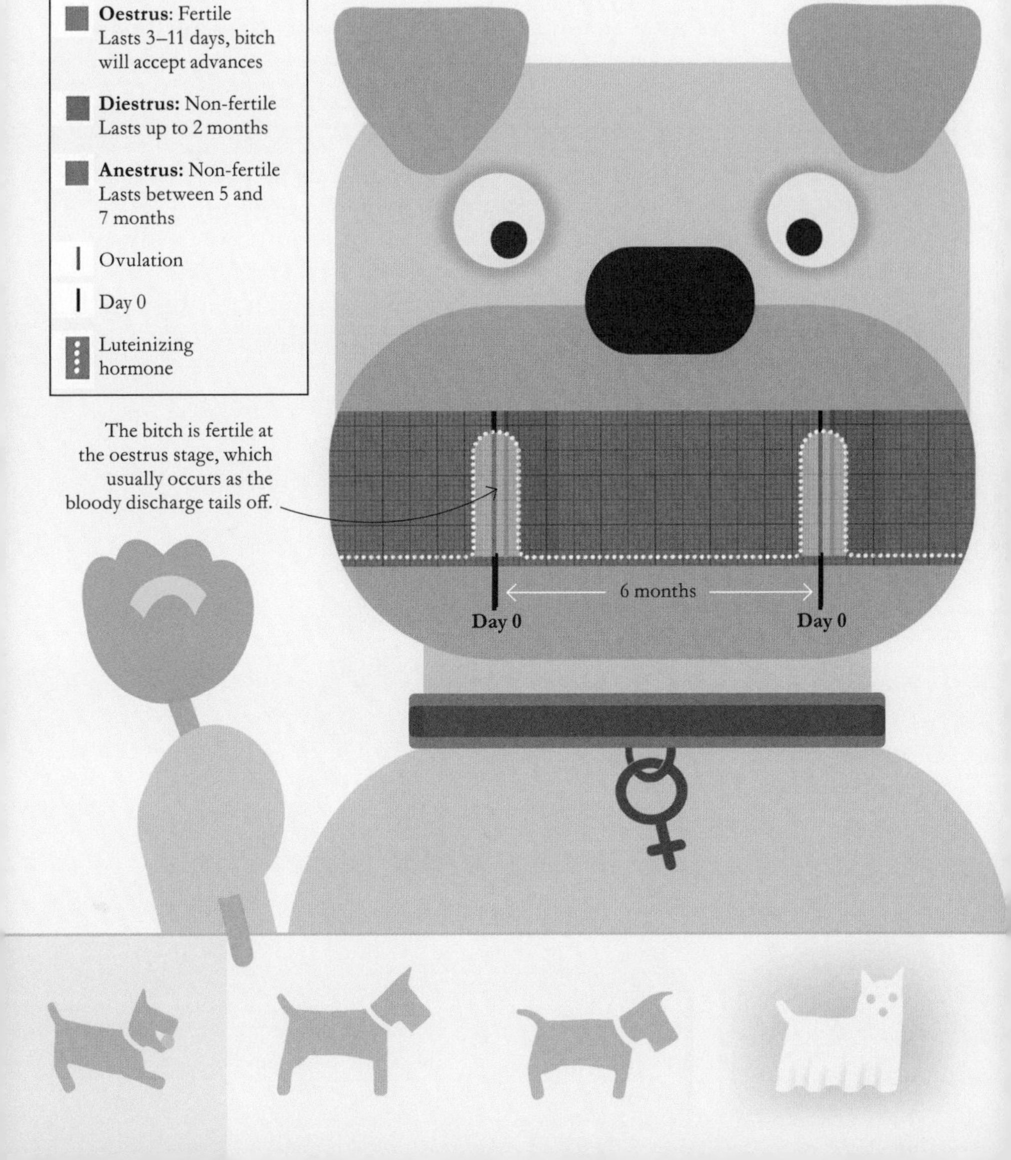

The bitch is fertile at the oestrus stage, which usually occurs as the bloody discharge tails off.

6 months

Day 0

Day 0

Adult

By the time a dog has reached two years it is fully grown both physically and mentally. There may be behavioural changes after this, but these will be to do with things that happen to the dog rather than any further growing up that it has to do. We've seen earlier (pages 30–31) what the average day is like for a dog and that routine kicks in here.

New tricks
It is not true that you can't teach old dogs new tricks, in fact it is the opposite and it's important to recognize that mature dogs need stimulation. In some ways this is more the case than for younger dogs, because for those whippersnappers everything is new.

Variety
For mature dogs it is easy to fall into a rut, but by trying new things they prosper physically and mentally. This may be new toys to play with, different games, or alternative routes to your everyday walk. Variety is the spice of life.

Part of the furniture
This is the longest phase of a dog's life and it is when they have become an essential part of their human family.

Their body clocks become attuned to the rhythms of the home; they know when the children are due home from school, and the adults are almost home from work. They are like a living breathing alarm clock when it's dinnertime, but most of all they always seem to know your mood.

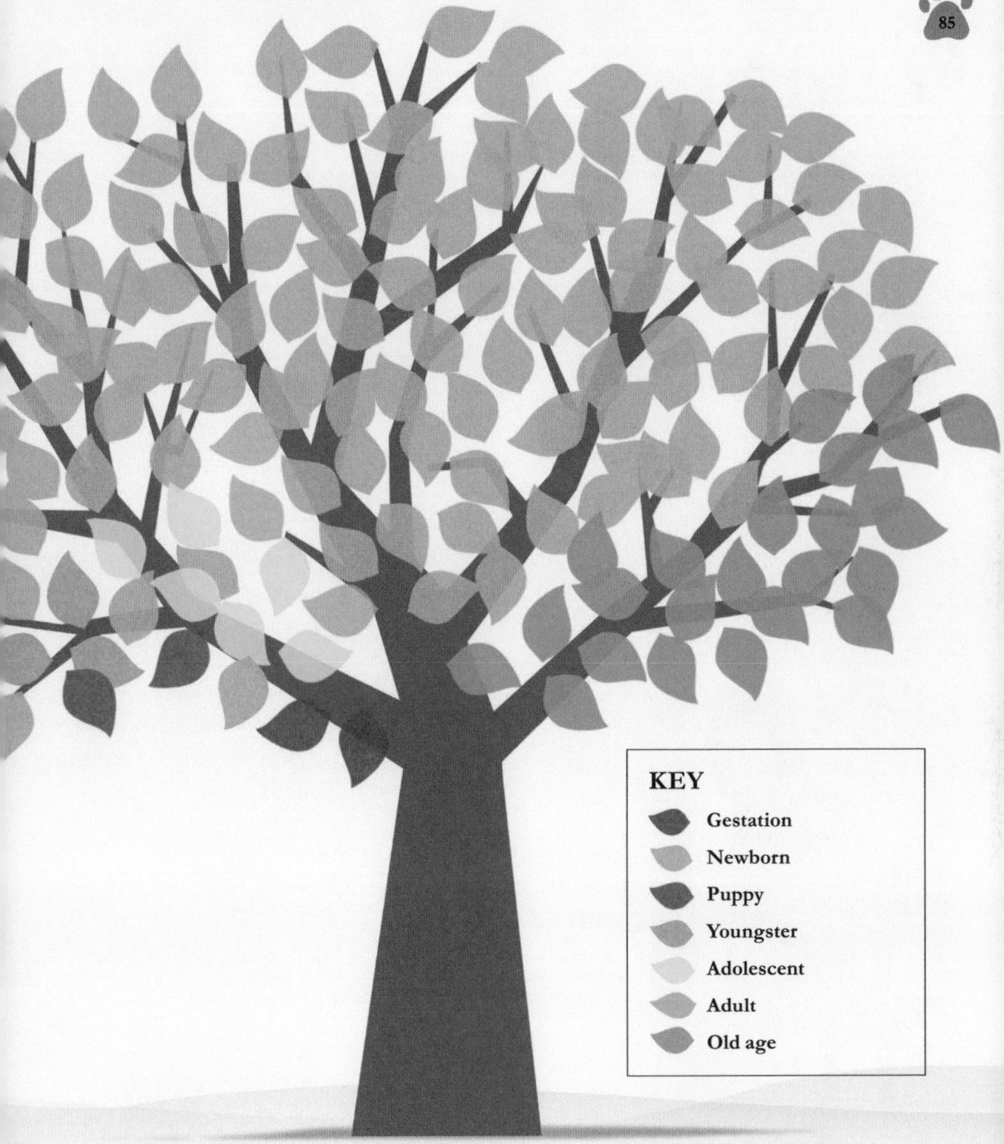

KEY

- Gestation
- Newborn
- Puppy
- Youngster
- Adolescent
- Adult
- Old age

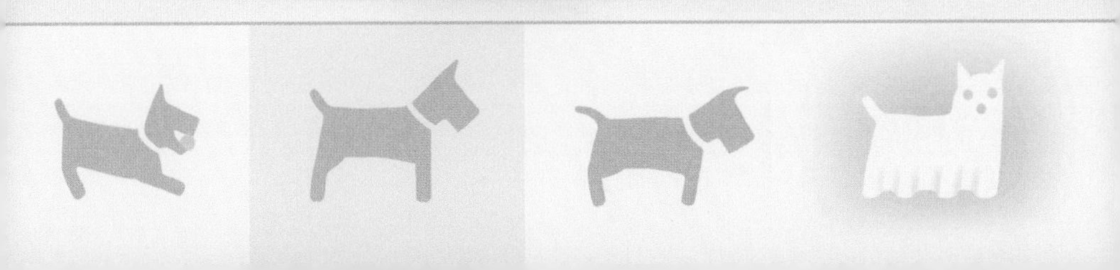

Old age

It happens to us all, unnoticed, but one day your dog will slow down. What was a one-hour walk now takes 75 minutes. Where she used to chase squirrels she now nods at them. What would have resulted in a vigorous chase with a dog now becomes a friendly chat.

Shorter walks

It's a part of life's cycle but you need to be aware of the changes. With less exercise, a dog's food will need to be reduced to avoid piling on the pounds. Your dog won't be able to jump up on to the sofa or fly up the stairs anymore, and a few short walks will replace one or two long treks. Mature dogs need exercise, but spread throughout the day.

More attention

The abilities a dog has relied on will start to go. Its sight, hearing, and sense of smell will deteriorate. It's important to be aware of this; your dog is not ignoring you, she may just not be able to hear, see, or smell you as easily as days gone by.

Older dogs can feel the cold more, will need more rest and more comfy bedding. They'll need to visit the loo more often! Senior dogs can enjoy long and happy final years, but it's like a return to the very early days where more attention is needed to make sure they are happy.

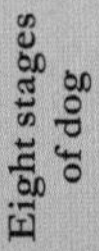

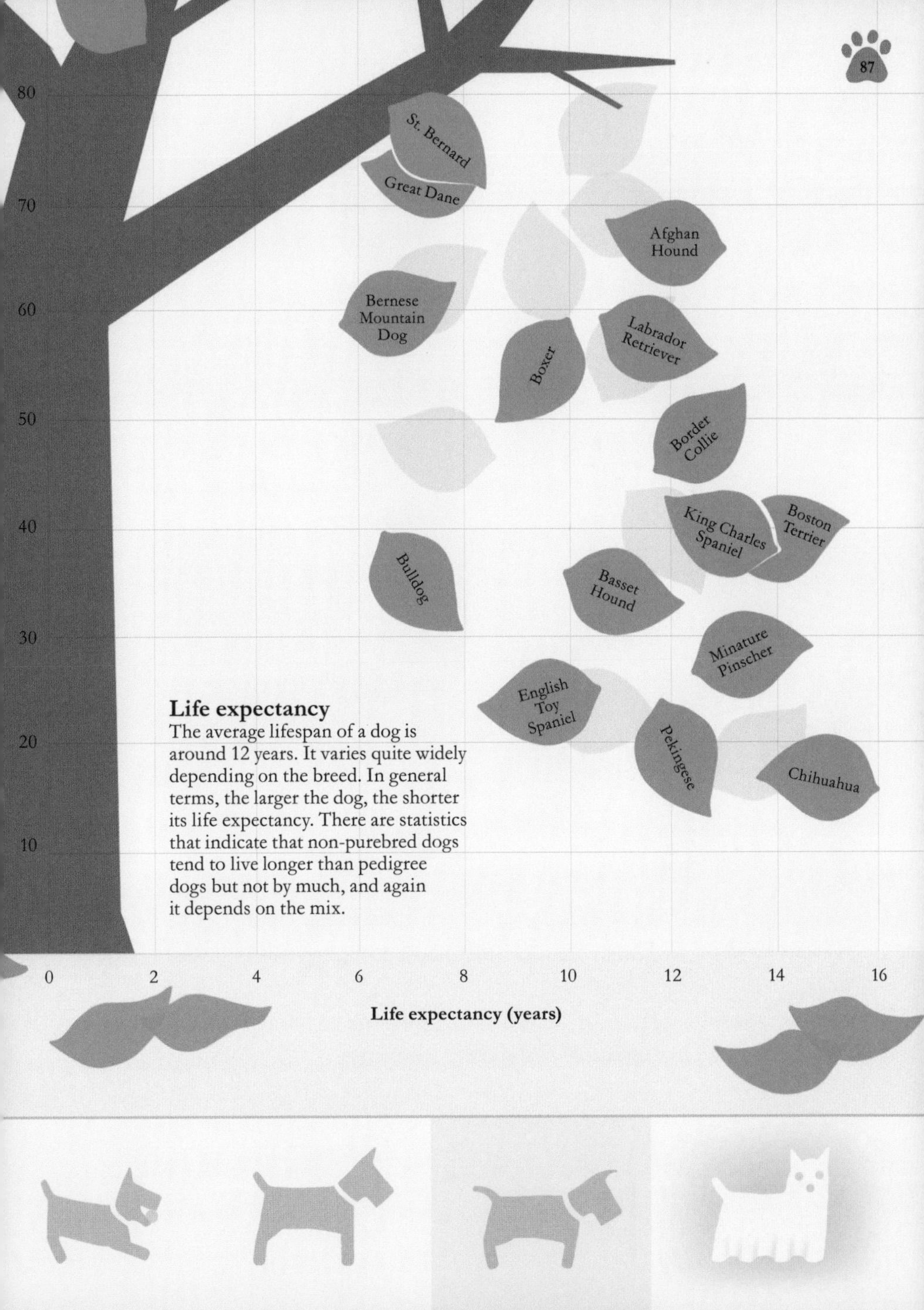

Life expectancy

The average lifespan of a dog is around 12 years. It varies quite widely depending on the breed. In general terms, the larger the dog, the shorter its life expectancy. There are statistics that indicate that non-purebred dogs tend to live longer than pedigree dogs but not by much, and again it depends on the mix.

The Ancient Egyptians believed that animals shared the afterlife, so pets were mummified and placed into tombs with their owners.

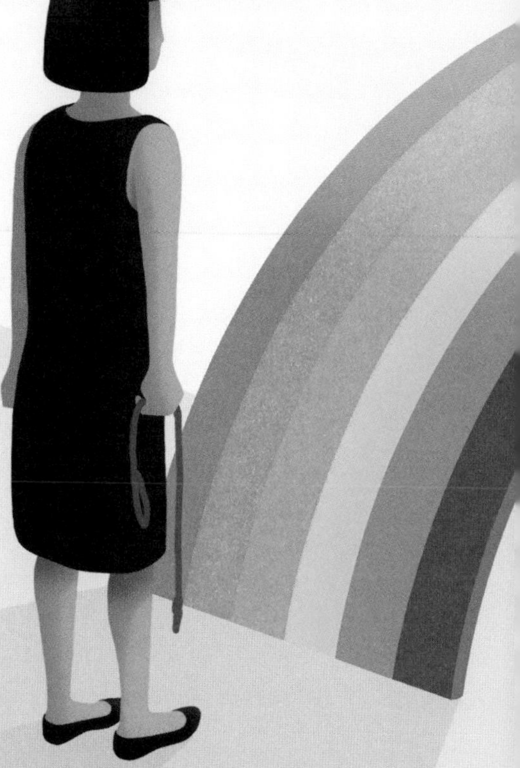

Rainbow Bridge

Dogs don't die. When their time comes they make their way to the Rainbow Bridge. There they are returned to their youthful glory; full of energy and spark. The sun shines, the fields are green, and fresh water runs in sparkling streams. Having fun with other dogs, there they will wait until they are reunited with their humans.

Eight stages of dog

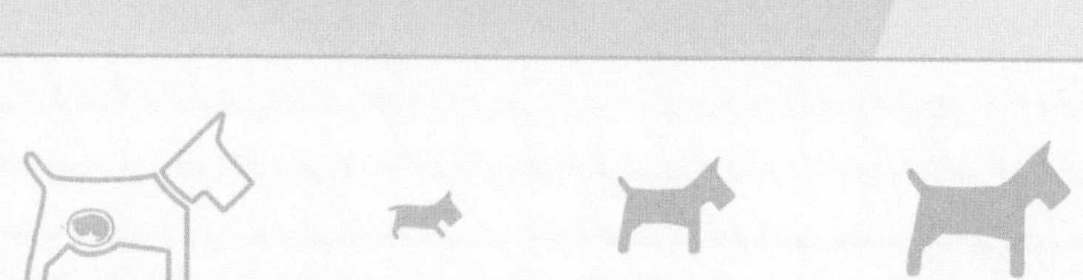

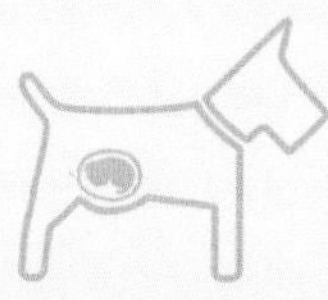

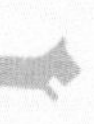

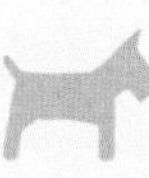

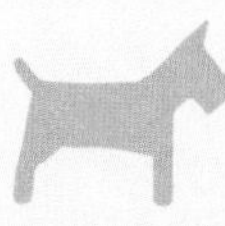

End of life

It's a comforting thought and since the Rainbow Bridge became a phenomenon in the 1980s, dog lovers everywhere have visualized it when their dog's days are done. The originator is disputed but what is not up for debate is that it is a comfort for their bereft families. In truth, dogs do die and as they are such an integral part of the family their passing is traumatic, but many see it as a good way for children to begin to understand mortality.

As well as breed, there are other factors that affect a dog's life expectancy. Diet, just as in humans, is very important. On average a dog that is neutered will live a few months longer. This difference is largely accounted for by the risks of cancer in intact dogs and bitches.

40% of dogs in the UK are buried in gardens

20% of funeral directors in the US offer dog funerals

Money can buy me love

In March 1964, The Beatles released their sixth single, the message of which was "money can't buy me love". The mop-top four had clearly never had a dog, but how much money does it take to keep your best friend in treats?

Upfront costs

The most expensive pedigree breeds can command a fee of almost £10,000 ($14,000) which is a lot, but in 2014 it was reported that a Tibetan Mastiff puppy sold for almost £1.5 million ($2 million)! If you're spending that much for your pooch then why not treat them well; Versace has made a food bowl which retails at over £500 ($750).

HOW MUCH IS THAT DOG?

The purchase price of your dog varies greatly around the world. Taking the supposed world's favourite dog, the Labrador, as an example you could pay as much as £2,300 ($3,200) in London but as little as £175 ($240) in Athens, Greece. In Beijing you'd pay around £360 ($500), which is similar to Madrid, while in New York and Toronto it would be in the region of £1,150 ($1,500).

This pile of money will disappear, replaced by love.

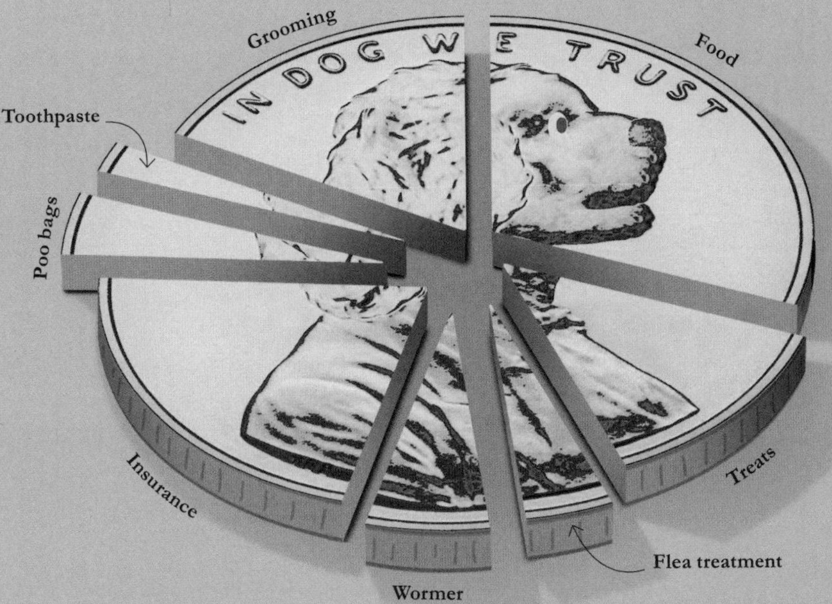

Monthly costs

On-going costs are things that need to be paid for throughout your dog's life. These figures are based on a monthly cost and may vary depending on the size and breed of the dog. There are other costs to consider. These are dependent on how you arrange your life around your dog and on things that may happen if you don't get pet insurance. Other costs include the following: dog walkers, day care, pet passport, boarding kennel, and neutering or spaying. Having a dog is a costly business, for a large breed it could add up to nearly £15,000 ($20,500) over its lifetime. That's a lot of poo bags!

Dogs with jobs

While most dogs are pets, it should not be forgotten that human's first relationship with them was a working one. The breed traits of many dogs still make them perfect to work alongside us. All over the world, dogs contribute to society in many ways, as well as being feet warmers on cold winter nights.

Dogs can help conservationists by sniffing for fresh whale poop, guiding research boats to where endangered species are.

Sniffer dogs

Police and military forces use dogs in their work in a variety of ways, such as crowd control, suspect arrests, and detection. So prevalent are dogs that some police forces call their specialist dog units K9! One of the most ubiquitous is the sniffer, or detection dog. With their incredibly sensitive noses, dogs can be trained to sniff out a variety of objects such as drugs and explosives and even human remains. One of most common breeds to be seen with a police officer is the German Shepherd because of its sense of smell, all-round abilities, and size.

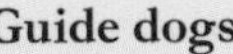

Guide dogs

The use of guide dogs owes its existence to a German doctor, Gerhard Stalling, who started training dogs to help soldiers blinded in World War I. The school, in the northwestern town of Oldenburg, expanded across the country and sent dogs around the world. Retrievers, Golden and Labrador, are the breed most commonly used for this work, mainly because of their trainability and mild temperament.

Search and rescue

When something bad happens it won't be long before a search and rescue dog is on the scene. They are used when disasters and accidents occur and people need to be found quickly. With their olfactory ability having been honed by training to sniff out human scent, they lead their handlers to the target. The first instances of the use of SAR dogs, as we now know them, was in World War I when they were used by the Red Cross to find injured soldiers on the battlefields. The Bloodhound has the best nose in the business.

Therapy dogs

The benefits of spending time with animals have been well documented ever since the founder of modern nursing, Florence Nightingale, first introduced the world to the concept of animal-assisted therapy in the late 1860s. The use of dogs to bring support, diversion, and invigoration grew rapidly through the 20th century. There isn't a specific breed that is best for therapy work, it is more to do with the personality of the individual dog and the training it has had.

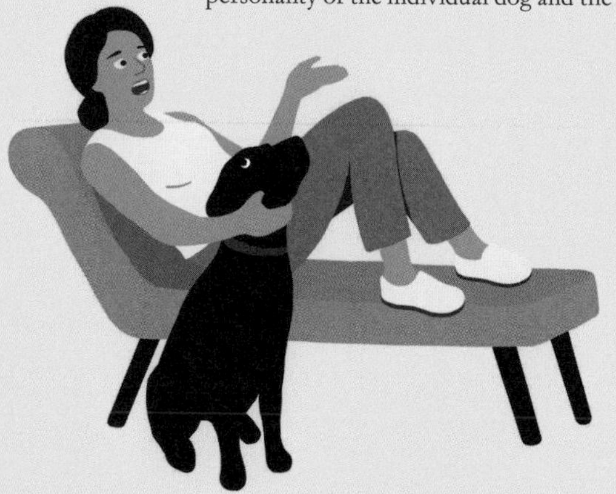

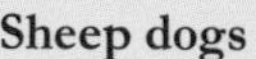

Sheep dogs

The term sheep dog covers both roles taken by dogs that work with sheep; herding and guarding. It is the herding role that is more skilled, requiring a range of abilities. Speed of thought and movement are high among these, as are attentiveness and concentration. There is debate about when and where sheepdog trials first became a competitive sport. Some claim it was 1867 in Wanaka, New Zealand, while others hold a flag for Bala, Wales, in 1873. Whichever it was, it has become a source of fierce rivalry and pride ever since. Border Collies are top of the heap as sheep dogs, combining excellently their speed, agility, attentiveness, and their use of a stare to control the flock.

Hearing dogs

While guide dogs for the blind have been around for a century, it was only in the 1970s that hearing dogs for the deaf came into being. Hearing dogs make sure that their human is made aware of their environment by alerting them to sounds around them. In the home, this can be things like alarms, doorbells, and mobile phones, while outdoors it is vehicles, other people, other dogs, and so on. As well as the expected Retrievers; Cocker Spaniels and Poodles make the best hearing dogs.

Sled dogs

For more than 9,000 years these dogs have worked the harshest conditions helping people travel in the Arctic and other places with arctic conditions! They work in teams dragging their load across the snow. With the invention of the snowmobile they are less used now, but sled racing has kept many occupied. The main breeds are the Alaskan Husky and Malamute, Canadian Inuit Dog, and the Samoyed.

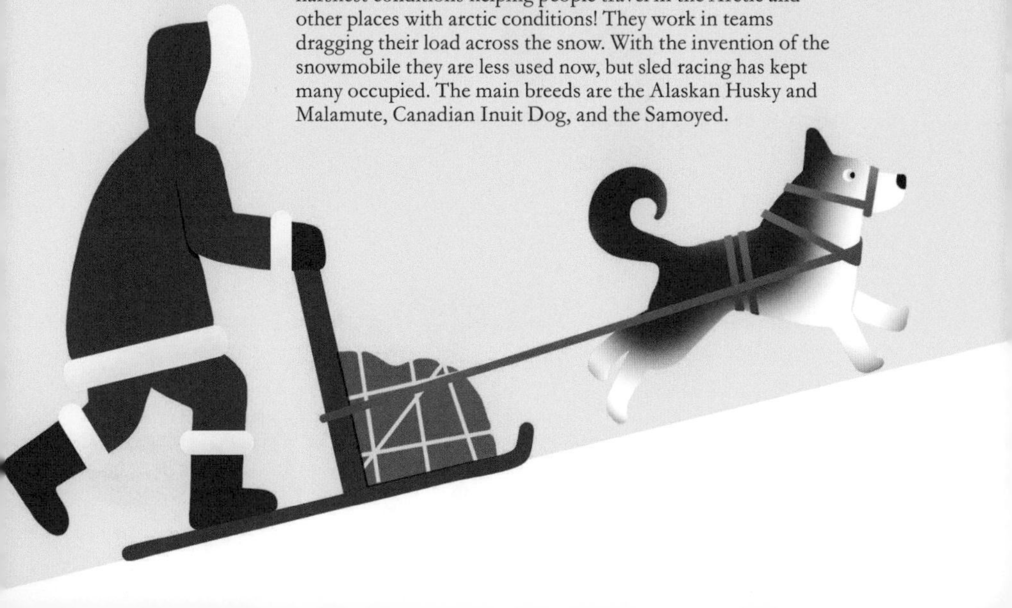

ON THE LEAD

When walking on the lead, it is important that you and your dog are moving at the same speed. This requires an equal amount of attention from both of you.

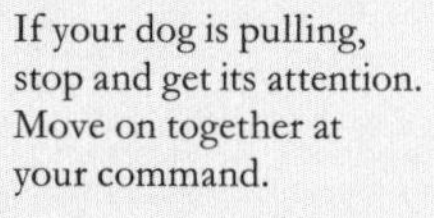
If your dog is pulling, stop and get its attention. Move on together at your command.

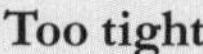
Too tight

If you're not walking at the same pace as your dog, the lead becomes a brake or a tow-line. Neither is good.

Too much slack

If the lead is too slack, your dog quickly forgets it is on the lead and will start doing its own thing.

Either let your dog off the lead, or decrease the slack.

Reward your dog to cement this good behaviour and keep the dog engaged.

Loose lead

Your dog is aware of the lead and you can use the lead for control if required.

OFF LEAD

When walking without a lead, the control you have over your dog as a result of good training replaces the physical connection.

Freedom

Being off lead gives your dog the chance to do what it wants, so at all times you must be attentive.

Dogs live in the moment. They do not plan ahead and they can't predict danger, so you have to do this for them.

How far is too far?

This varies from dog to dog and human to human. It depends how good your dog's recall is and how much you trust your dog when out of your sight.

Who's walking whom?

Michel de Montaigne was a 16th-century French philosopher. One of his most famous thoughts was, "When I am playing with my cat, how do I know she is not playing with me?" It's a train of thought that many people must have had when walking their dog. You put the lead on the dog but you are on the other end – so who is walking whom?

Walking to heel

This is when your dog walks right by you and is best used if there are dangers nearby, such as roads or picnics!

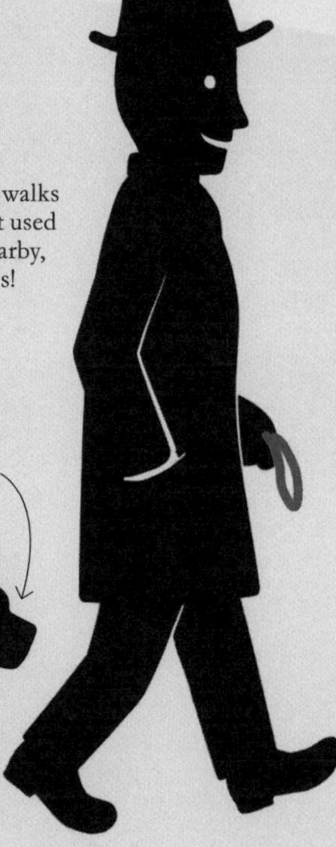

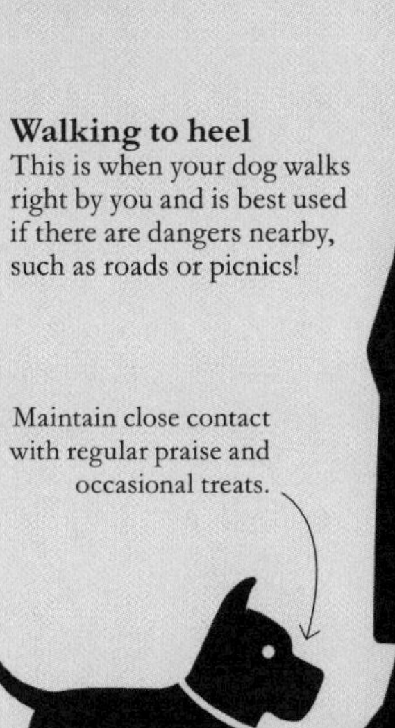

Maintain close contact with regular praise and occasional treats.

Throwing a sickie

Dogs can't tell us when they are ill. This means we have to monitor them to make sure that any problem can be investigated as soon as possible. Here are some of the subtle things we should look out for.

BEHAVIOUR

We spend a lot of time with our dog and know the sorts of things they do during a normal day. This should make it quite easy to spot when your dog's behaviour changes.

Don't be tempted to plug your dog into a recharger.

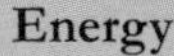

Energy

A change in your dog's energy is a good clue that something may be wrong. Are they playing less, running less, generally a little rundown?

The bum drag

Most dog owners will see the bum scoot at some stage. If you don't know what it is it actually looks quite funny, but it's not. It normally means something is irritating your dog's bottom.

This brown line does not actually appear.

Strange reaction to stroking or cuddling

If your dog has an internal injury or a damaged bone, they will react when you try to touch them in that area.

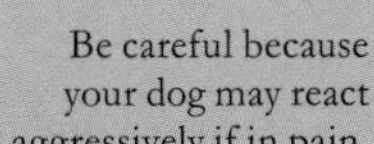

Be careful because your dog may react aggressively if in pain.

Never poke anything into a dog's ear to try to extricate what is stuck.

Excessive head shake

The head shake can be part of normal behaviour, but should only be seen occasionally. What you need to look out for is when your dog is doing it much more than a couple of times a week. This may mean they have something stuck in their ear or an infection.

DIGESTION

The early days of human medicine put a lot of store in checking what came out the other end of our digestive system, and it's a good thing to do with your dog.

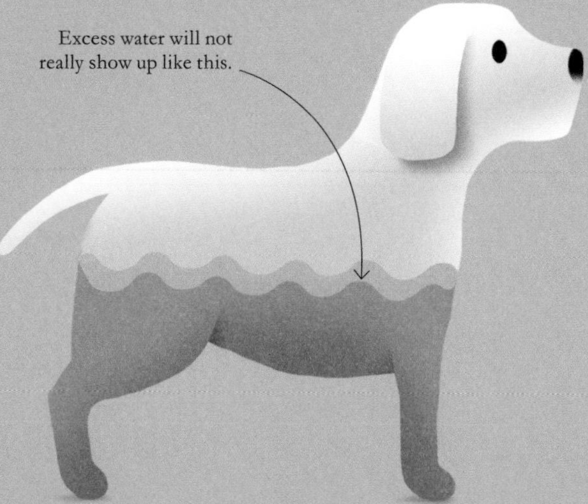

Excess water will not really show up like this.

Drinking a lot more than usual

This is tricky to monitor as you may not be around to see your dog drink, but if you notice that you're having to fill up the water bowl a lot more than usual then there may be a problem.

Loss of appetite

A sure sign of an unwell dog is that they go off their food. This is very rare so can be serious.

This is not a wizard's hat.

Vomiting

Dogs can end up eating a lot of strange things on their walks, especially when they are out of sight. Sometimes these will go straight through, sometimes they come out the way they went in. The danger signs are if your dog vomits repeatedly or if there is blood in the vomit.

Unusually coloured urine

We know ourselves that if we haven't drunk enough our wee looks a lot darker. It's the same with dogs.

Look out especially for blood.

This is a simulation.

Poo

Is it runny, are there worms in it, is there blood in it? When you pick up your dog's poo have a look at it to see if there is anything that shouldn't be there. It's also worth noting if your dog is having to try harder than normal to poo!

SKIN AND BONES

They say you can't judge a book by its cover, but that is not the case with dogs. Checking out their skin, fur, and bones is a useful indicator of health.

Fur

Any changes in the look or feel of your dog's fur should be monitored.

Gait

If your dog gets something stuck in its paw it will walk differently. This will also happen if it has a problem with its bones or muscles.

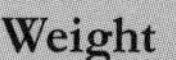

Weight

You should regularly weigh your dog. A sudden loss of a lot of weight could be a sign that something is wrong.

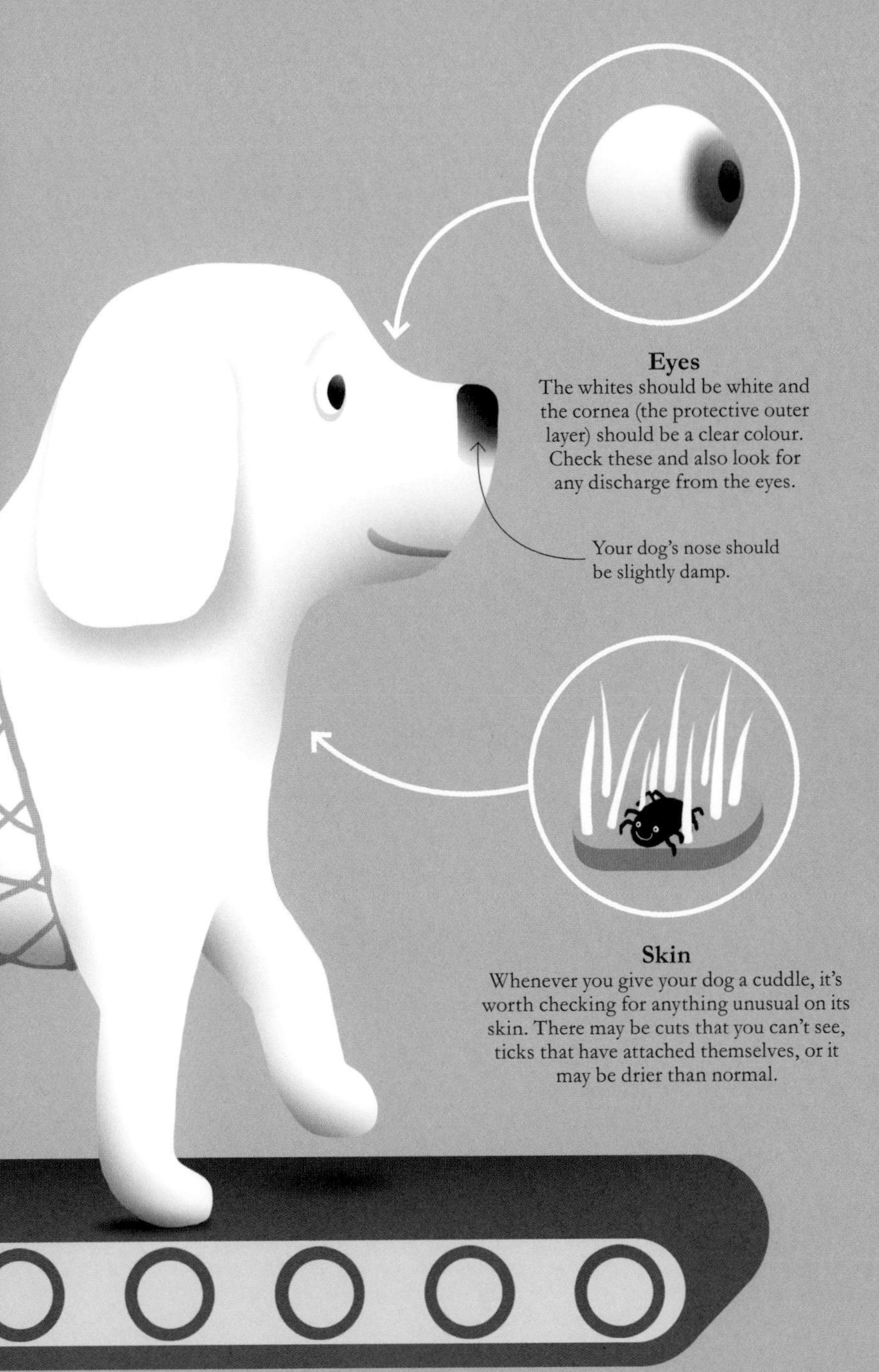

Eyes

The whites should be white and the cornea (the protective outer layer) should be a clear colour. Check these and also look for any discharge from the eyes.

Skin

Whenever you give your dog a cuddle, it's worth checking for anything unusual on its skin. There may be cuts that you can't see, ticks that have attached themselves, or it may be drier than normal.

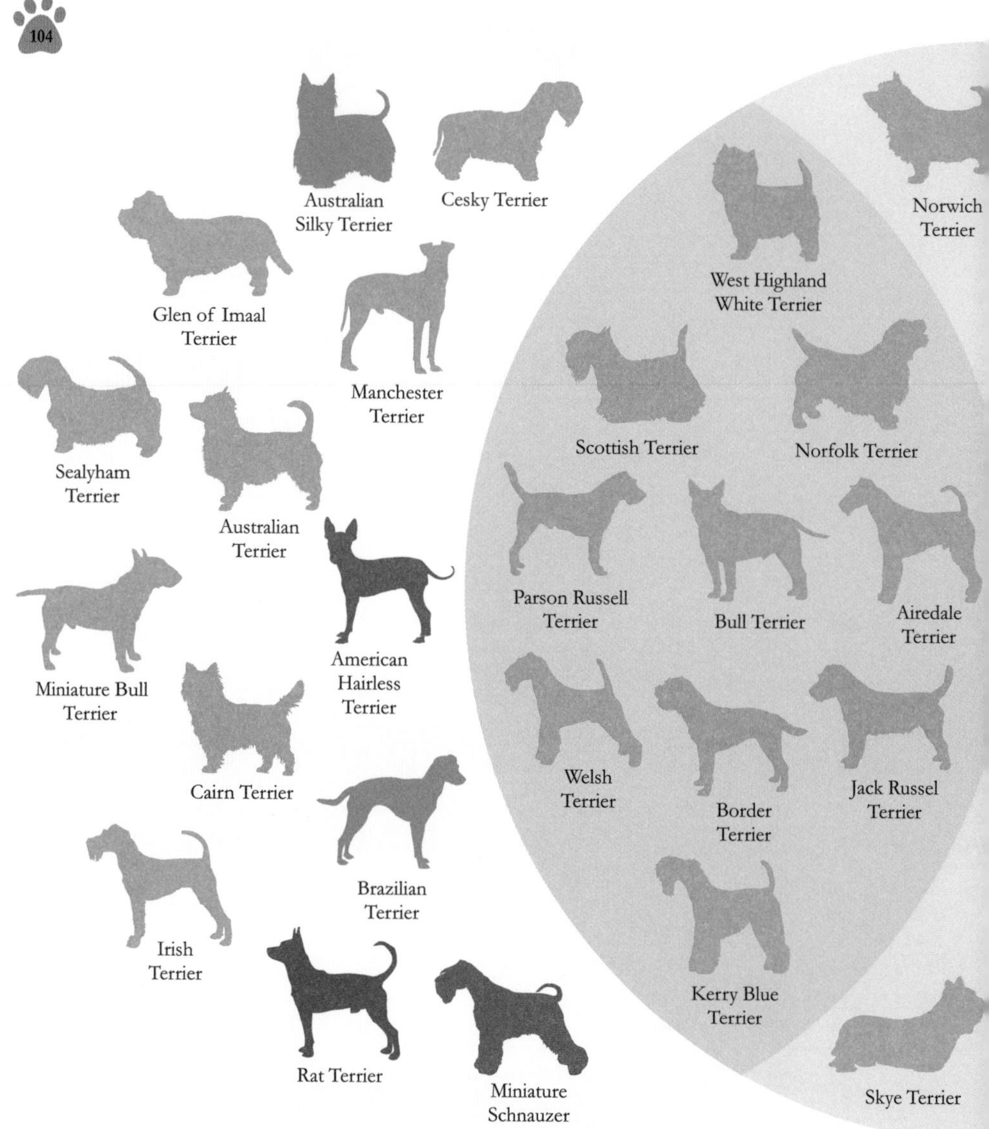

THREE TYPES

The terrier group can be divided into three: working, toy, and bull. The working terriers are the original hunters, the toys are larger breeds bred down in size as companions. The bull-types have come from cross-breeding with bulldogs, often for fighting which, thankfully, is now banned in most countries.

Terriers

Terriers were bred to hunt and kill mice, rats, and other small vermin. The word comes from the Latin *Terra*, meaning earth. They chase prey down holes and never give up, hence terrier has become synonymous with tenacity. They are sturdy and energetic, like a pocket battleship with fur. As the hunting they were bred for is mainly solitary they need to be well socialized to get on with other dogs.

Soft-coated Wheaten Terrier

Yorkshire Terrier

German Hunting Terrier

Fox Terrier

Bedlington Terrier

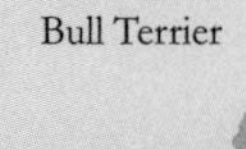

Staffordshire Bull Terrier

Lakeland Terrier

Dandie Dinmont Terrier

American Staffordshire Terrier

Japanese Terrier

KEY

Original use:

Vermin hunter

Small game hunter

Non-hunters

Which clubs they belong to:

American Kennel Club (AKC)

Fédération Cynologique Internationale (FCI)

AKC and FCI

The Kennel Club, AKC, and FCI

STAFFIE POPULARITY

The Staffordshire Bull Terrier seems to be an extreme example of a Marmite dog; either very well loved or not at all. With a high weight to strength ratio this breed was originally used for blood sports, but paradoxically is also popular as a family pet. The thing is that they look a little scary but are actually very friendly.

How it ranks

These rosettes show how the Staffordshire Bull Terrier ranks in popularity compared to other breeds. There is no middle ground wherever the Staffie is found; top of the tree or down in the dumps.

Dandie Dinmont Terrier

The Dandie Dinmont has to be one of the best names of all the breeds. It comes from a character in Sir Walter Scott's novel *Guy Mannering*, published in 1815. Dandie Dinmont was a farmer in this tale of smugglers, the second of the Waverley novels.

Fox Terrier

The Fox Terriers, both smooth and wire-haired, were very popular in the first half of the 20th century, but in recent years they have fallen out of favour. There's no obvious reason for this, although it could be that they have such high energy and not every family can cope.

Border Terrier

Some dogs are born half-trained, but it is often said of Border Terriers that they die half-trained. They're intelligent and sturdy but have an independent streak that makes them a feisty test for anyone. Their friendly demeanour and funny old-man faces more than make up for any downside this causes. The perfect dog.*

*Yes, the author is the support team to a border terrier.

Cock-a-poodle-do

Crossbreeding was first done to combine the desired characteristics of two different pure breeds. Initially, this was only done for working purposes, but now it is mostly done for aesthetic reasons or the health considerations of potential owners, such as coats that don't shed for allergy sufferers. It is possible for any breeds to be crossed, although there are physical restrictions when attempting to do this naturally.

Male Breed A + Female Breed B = Crossbreed AB

What is a crossbreed?

Crossbreed AB may not always turn out the same – even in one litter – and the outcome is unpredictable. It is not as simple as making a cake, for instance, where you can measure the ingredients to get consistent results. It shouldn't matter which is male and which is female in terms of how the offspring look and behave, but generally the male will be the smaller of the two to avoid complications with the birth.

Pure breeds

To be classed as a pure breed, the offspring must always exhibit the anticipated characteristics of the parents. They should be true to type.

Male Breed A + Female Breed A = Breed A

Crossbreeds become pure breeds

The process can take a long time, as the breed standard needs to be set and recorded for a number of years to establish it as a distinct new breed.

Male Crossbreed AB + Female Crossbreed AB = Breed AB

More than one crossbreed

It can get more complicated if the crossbreed is a mixture of more than two pure breeds! An extreme example is the Black Russian Terrier, created in the 1950s by the Red Star Kennel of the Soviet Union (see page 129) from up to 17 different breeds and now a recognized breed.

Male Crossbreed ABC + Female Crossbreed DEF = Breed ABCDEF?

HISTORIC CROSSBREEDS

One of the earliest crossbreeds is the Lurcher, which dates back to 14th-century England, when commoners were not entitled to own purebred hounds but poachers would cross their dogs with the lord's Greyhounds. It is still not recognized as a pure breed today.

Lurcher

This hunting dog is a cross between a sighthound, of which there are 16 breeds, and another dog – often a Terrier, combining speed and tenacity.

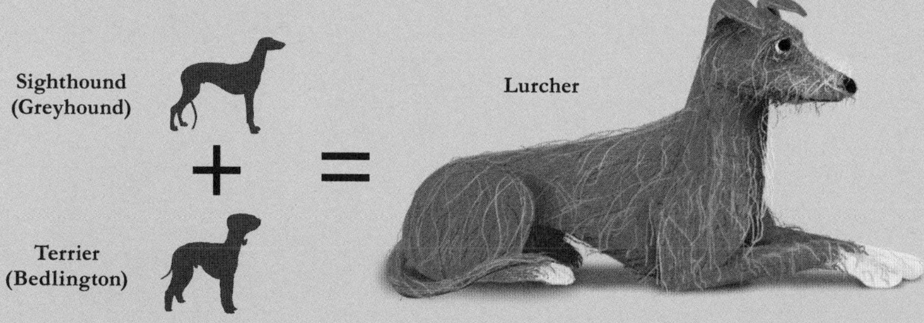

POPULAR CROSSBREEDS

With the explosion of social media, the speed with which a crossbreed becomes popular has increased exponentially. It only takes one mega-celebrity to turn up on a red carpet for a new crossbreed to become the flavour of the month.

Malshi

Possibly the most popular non-Poodle cross, the Maltese-Shih Tzu mix is also referred to as the Malshi and is a low fur-shedder.

Dobermann

Karl Friedrich Louis Dobermann was a German tax collector who also ran a dog pound. He wanted a dog that was loyal, strong, clever, and scary to help him with his day job. Over a short period of time he was able to produce the Dobermann, which was first recognized as a pure breed in 1908.

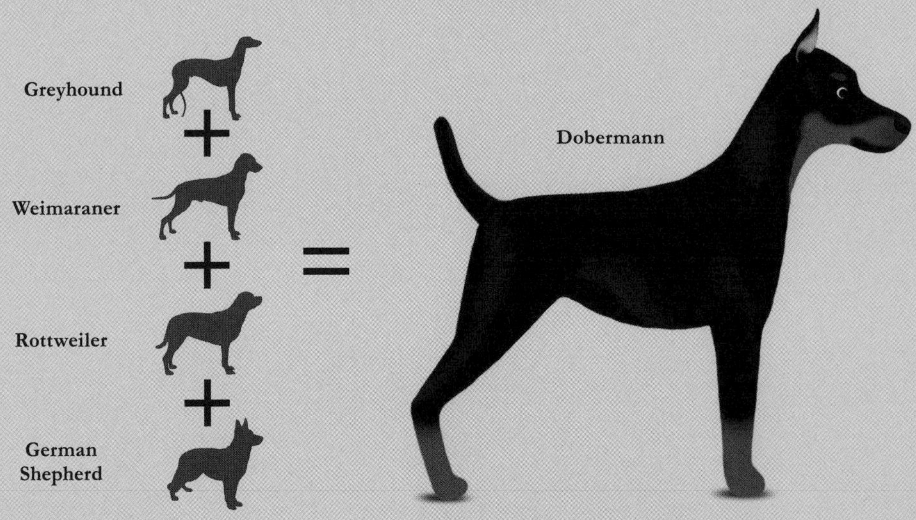

Labradoodle

This Labrador–Poodle cross is popular with people who have allergies and want a good-natured dog. The poodle's coat is a low-shedder and the Labrador is reputed for its temperatment. First seen in the 1950s, it was popularized in Australia in the late 1980s.

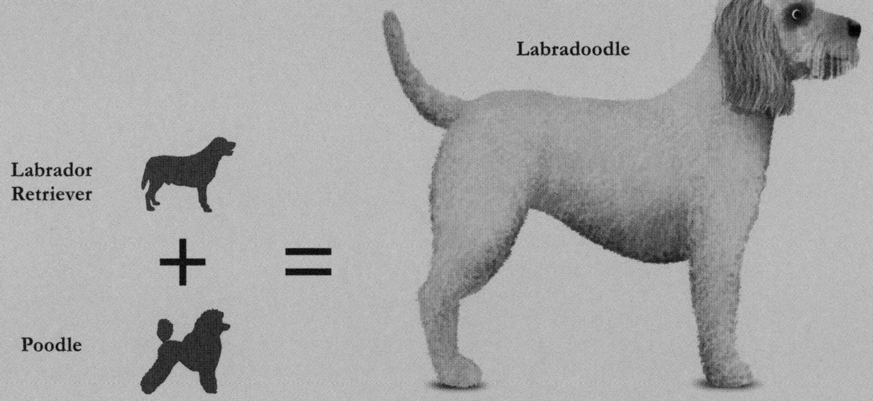

Hairstyles

There is no such thing as bad weather, only bad clothing. While you can buy clothing for dogs, it isn't really necessary because they already have the best coat possible. It keeps them warm in winter and cool in the summer, and protects them from all sorts of dangers. Of course we humans love to interfere. Here's a small selection of the most iconic barnets. The examples here are all show cuts.

Poodle

The most distinctive and recognizable hairstyle at any show, it gives poodles an air of distinction and means that they are often mistaken for overly pampered dogs. But this style comes from a working practicality. The bare hips and legs were to allow for swimming freedom, while the volume was for warmth and to aid buoyancy for this water dog.

Scottish Terrier

This terrier has a very recognizable silhouette which comes mainly from the head shape. The Scottie is the breed on which the Monopoly board game dog is based. The squarer "beard" came into fashion in the early 1900s and the longer coat, down to the ground, followed in middle of the 20th century.

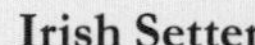

Irish Setter

Often called the Red Setter because of the colour of its coat, this breed is easily spotted at a distance thanks to the colour and shine of its fur as well as the cut. It is cut short on its head and forelegs, and kept longer and silky elsewhere. Because the Irish Setter's hair is so silky and long it needs regular brushing to avoid knotting. This should be done at least three times a week.

Pekingese

No one is quite sure what this breed looks like under its coat. If ever there was a dog that is defined by its hair, this is it. Small in stature but top of the game when it comes to hairstyle swagger, the Pekingese is a coat on legs, not that you can see them.

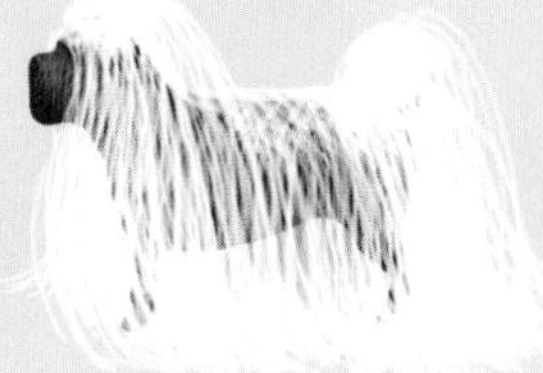

Shih Tzu

With its extravagant double coat and top-knot, this is a look that turns heads wherever it is seen. The style is long and requires regular maintenance – more than one brushing a day. Shih Tzus can be seen away from the show ring with much shorter, more manageable cuts that make them look like a totally different dog.

Spot that dog

A number of breeds have spots on their coats; Cocker Spaniels, Springer Spaniels, and Border Collies to name just three. The list goes to over 20, but there is only one dog that is known specifically for its spots and that is the Dalmatian.

Originating from Dalmatia, a strip of land along the coast of modern-day Croatia, the Dalmatian has one of the most distinctive coats of any breed. Made world famous by the Disney film *101 Dalmatians*, this regal dog is classified as Utility/Non-Sporting by The Kennel Club and the American Kennel Club, while the FCI has it as a Scenthound.

Changing names

It has been known by a number of different names mainly linked to jobs it has had over the centuries. For a long time it was a Carriage or Spotted Coach Dog because it accompanied and protected the horses that pulled the coaches. In the US, it fulfilled a similar task alongside horse-drawn fire engines, earning the epithet Firehouse Dog.

In the States it was also closely associated with Budweiser beer as their wagons would be seen all over the country with a Dalamatian in attendance.

Unique spots

Dalmatian puppies are born pure white all over, the spots only appearing after around three weeks. The spots should be circular and the most prized examples have non-overlapping spots. As well as being a striking look, the spotted coats of the Dalmatian are as unique as fingerprints. This is why it's very rare for Dalmatians to turn to crime as they are so easily singled out.

Other coat patterns

While the Dalmatian coat is the best known, other styles are available.

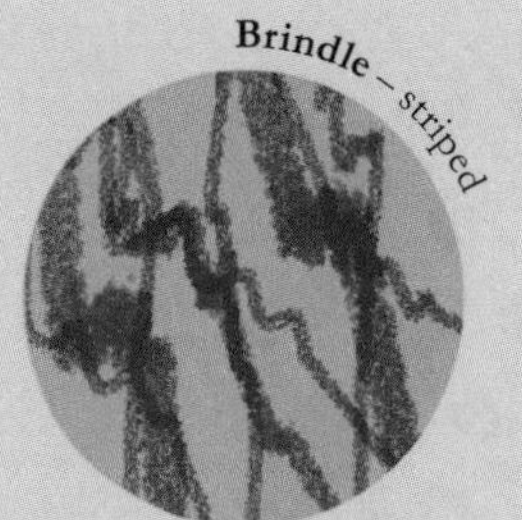

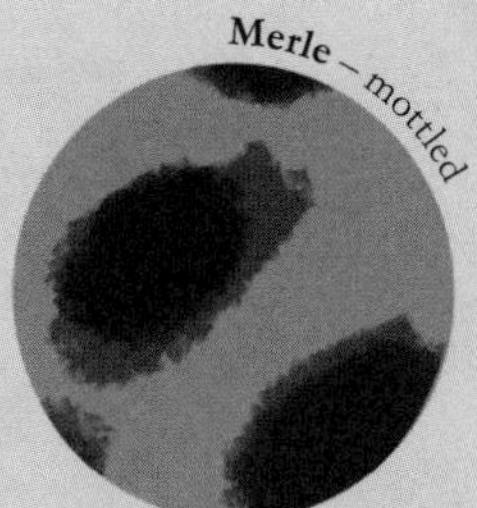

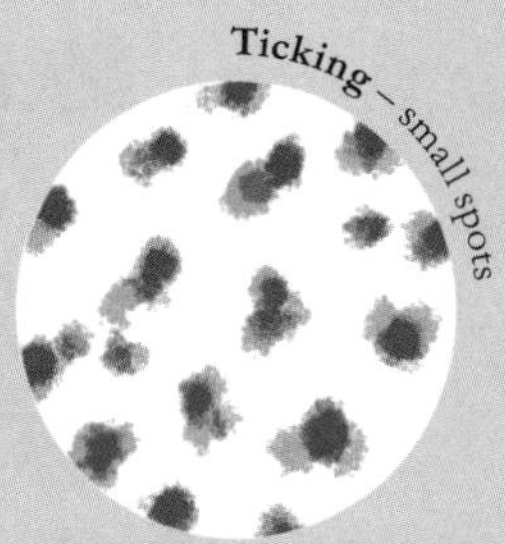

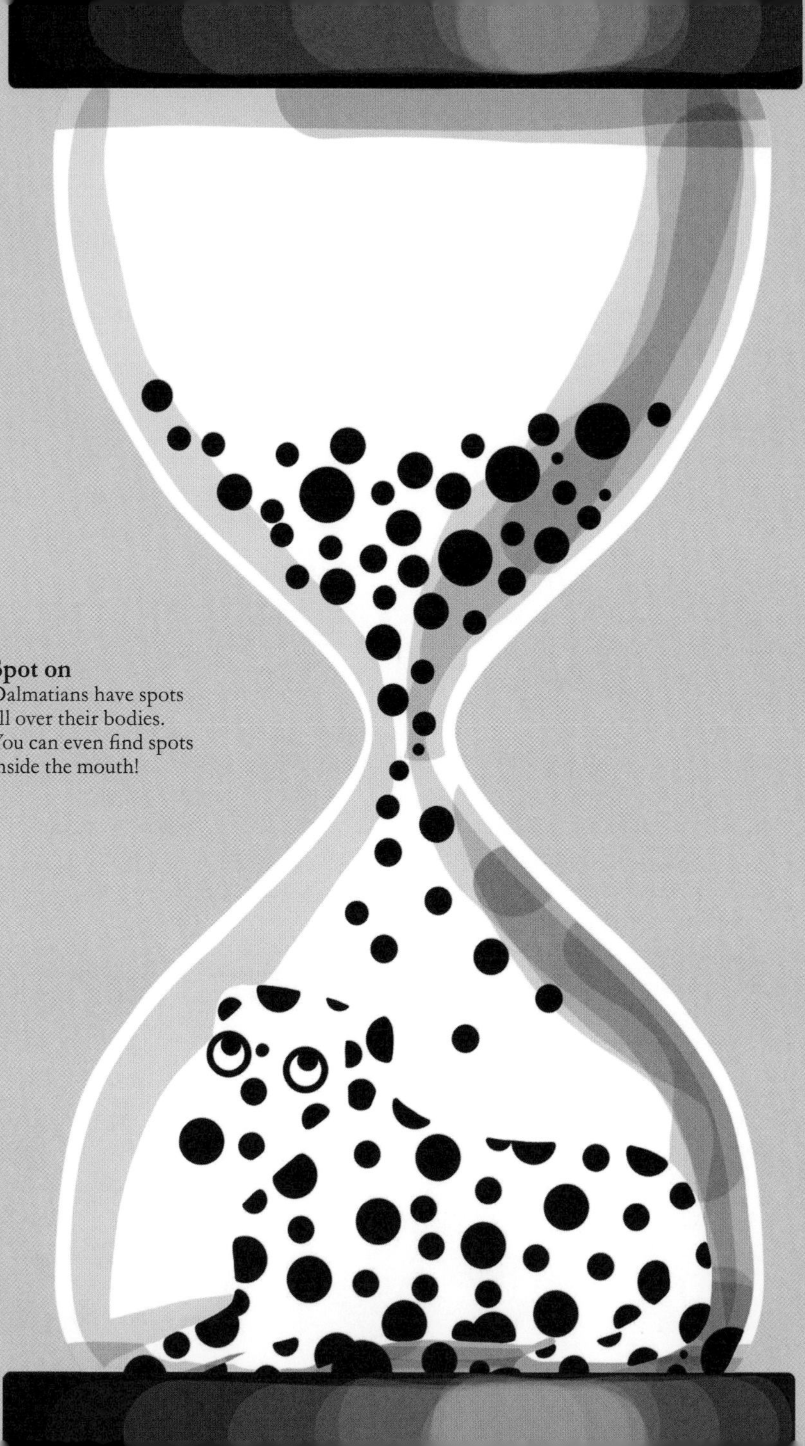

Spot on
Dalmatians have spots all over their bodies. You can even find spots inside the mouth!

Superdog

Crossbreeding takes the best elements of two dogs and tries to combine them into one even better dog, but what if you could go further and take the best characteristics of several dogs and combine it into one Superdog. What would it look like?

Temperament – Labrador Retriever
The American Temperament Test Society conducts research based on dogs' constancy, timidity, hostility, and affability as well as each dog's instinct to defend its owner.

Speed – Greyhound
Reaching speeds of more than 70 km/h (43 mph), greyhounds are the fastest dogs. That's quick enough to cover 30 m (98 ft) in 1 second.

Stamina – Alaskan Malamute
Not surprisingly, the most resilient dogs are a working breed, specifically bred for pulling heavy loads in tough conditions.

Hearing – Miniature Pinscher
Dogs can hear a wider range of frequencies than we do. The Miniature Pinscher's ability to swivel its ears independently enhances its hearing even further.

Brains – Border Collie
Bred to herd sheep and cattle, the Border Collie is recognized as the smartest dog in the field. It is easy to train, quick to learn, and able to understand a range of commands.

Sight – Whippet
Sighthounds hunt by sight rather than scent. It is a feature of their eyes that holds the secret: the retina has a streak of vision cells more sensitive than in other dogs. This increases the clarity of their peripheral vision so they can detect movement more accurately.

Smell – Bloodhound
With a sense of smell at least 100 times that of humans, scent is the special skill that really sets dogs apart – and the bloodhound has the best nose of them all.

Bite – Turkish Kangal
This pastoral dog is used to guard livestock and has a bite strength that is more than four times as strong as that of the average human.

NOTABLE OMISSIONS

It's worth noting that this group does not include some obvious working types such as the herding breeds. These can be found in the Pastoral group.

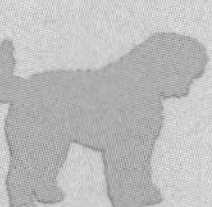

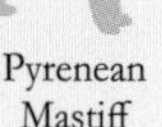

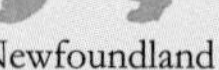

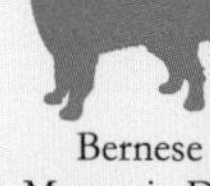

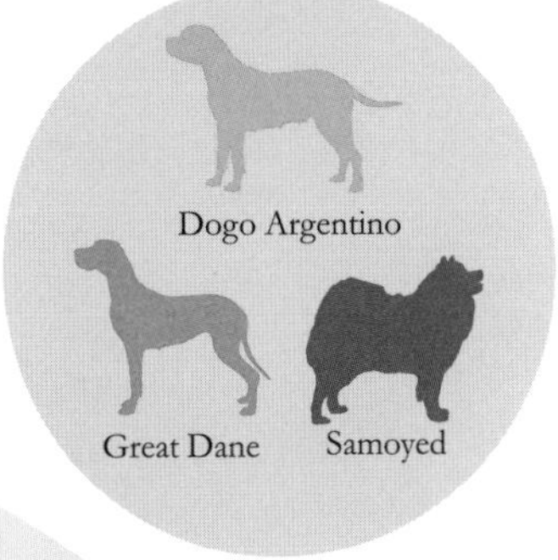

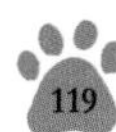

Dogo Argentino
Great Dane
Samoyed

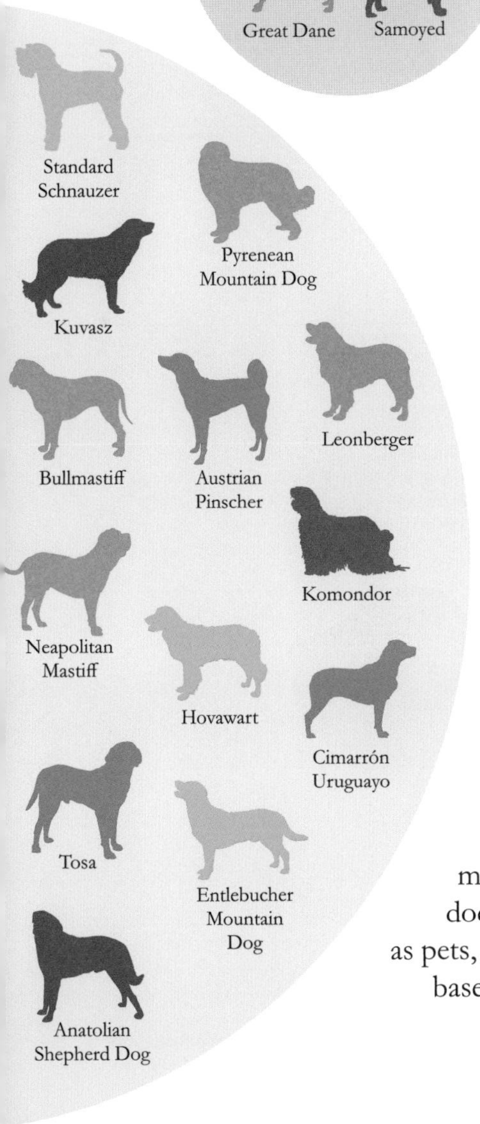

Standard Schnauzer
Pyrenean Mountain Dog
Kuvasz
Leonberger
Bullmastiff
Austrian Pinscher
Komondor
Neapolitan Mastiff
Hovawart
Cimarrón Uruguayo
Tosa
Entlebucher Mountain Dog
Anatolian Shepherd Dog

KEY

Job suitablility:

- Military and police
- Rescue
- Sledging and hauling
- Guarding
- None of the above

Which clubs they belong to:

- The Kennel Club (TKC)
- American Kennel Club (AKC)
- Fédération Cynologique Internationale (FCI)
- TKC and AKC
- AKC and FCI
- TKC, AKC, and FCI

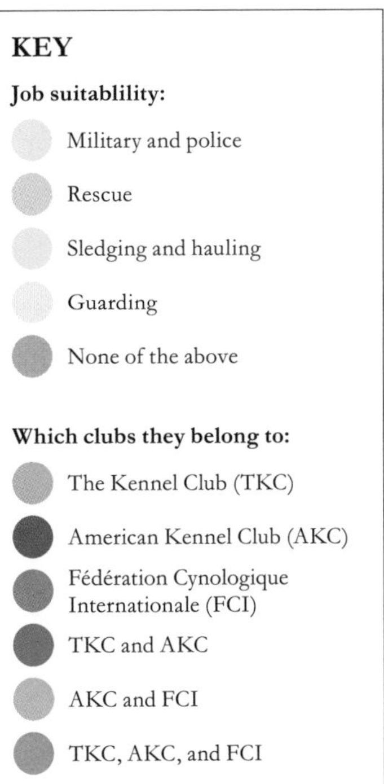

Working dogs

As the name suggests, this group is made up of dogs with a job to do. That doesn't mean that they will not be taken as pets, but their original breed standard was based on the specific requirements of the work they were needed to do.

Working dog sizes

All of the dogs currently classified in this group are either large or medium in size, with most being the former. These are sturdy, muscular dogs who take well to training and have a good level of concentration. Most military and police dogs will come from this group, as well as those used for guarding and pulling heavy loads such as sledging dogs.

Most of the breeds in this group are big to huge and, partly because of this, it is no surprise that most dogs deemed "dangerous" come from this group. Dogs are not dangerous per se but when they are mishandled, untrained, or badly trained they can be. And when they are big those dangers can become fatal which is why a number of dogs in this group are banned in various countries.

Boxer

The Boxer was widely used on both sides globally in the military during the two world wars, but it was only after World War II that the breed became widely popular. This was in part because soldiers brought them home after the conflict and kept them as pets.

Black Russian Terrier

The Black Russian Terrier is a product of the Soviet Red Star Kennels (see page 129). While the nickname for a dog with an unknown heritage is a Heinz 57, this breed is believed to have been the product of input from a mere 17 breeds.

ROTTWEILER VS DOBERMANN

Ali vs Frasier, Godzilla vs King Kong, Tom vs Jerry; everywhere you look there are iconic match ups and the same is true of the Rottweiler and the Dobermann. Not a fight of course, just a popularity contest.

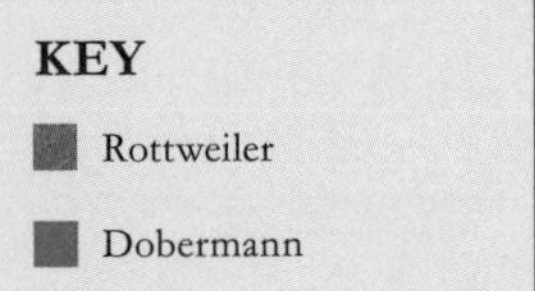

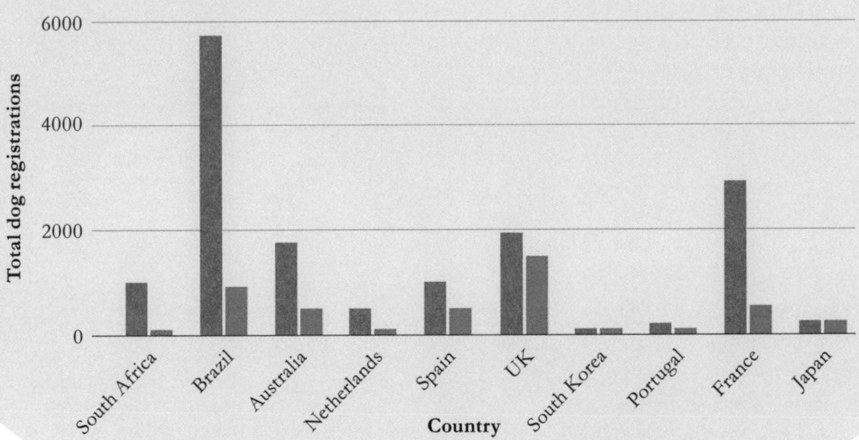

Dogue de Bordeaux

The Dogue de Bordeaux has been around in France since the 14th century when it was a guard dog, but the breed was only officially recognized by TKC in 1997. Because of its huge size – males weigh over 65 kilos (140 lb) – it was used in the past as a fighting dog against bulls and bears. In spite of their size, when raised properly they are a relaxed breed and make good family pets.

Dogs on screen

In 2001, Otis won Cannes' Palm Dog for *The Anniversary Party*. A pun on the festival's main prize, this goes to the best performance by a dog. Since Jean, the first dog star, appeared in 25 films between 1910 and 1915, stories about dogs have become common. Pooches often upstage the humans, hence W.C. Fields advising, "Never work with animals or children".

KEY

The author has awarded each dog a star rating out of five for its screen appeal, based on a range of criteria.

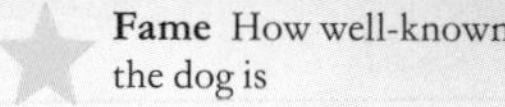

Fame How well-known the dog is

Heroism In honour of heroic acts carried out by the dog

Films How many films the dog star or character appears in

Recognition Unprompted awareness of the dog's name

Star Quality A measure of the dog's glamour and magnetism

Rough Collie

LASSIE

English novelist Eric Knight's Yorkshire-set novel *Lassie Come-Home* was published in 1940. It takes the reader along with Lassie as she tries to find her master, young Jack Carraclough, after she has been sold. This was the only book Knight wrote about Lassie, but it led to more than 10 films, a long-running television series, and several animated series, which made the Collie a household name around the world.

Fame	★★★★★
Heroism	★★★★★
Films	★★★★★
Recognition	★★★☆☆
Star Quality	★★★★☆

UGGIE

Uggie's first named role was opposite stars Robert Pattinson and Reece Witherspoon in the romcom *Water for Elephants* in 2011, but he found worldwide fame in the silent French comedy *The Artist* in the same year. His starring role as Jack alongside comic actor Jean Dujardin led to a campaign for the Academy Awards to give him a special award, but he had to make do with the Palm Dog.

Parson Russell Terrier

Fame	★★★★☆
Heroism	★★☆☆☆
Films	★☆☆☆☆
Recognition	★★★☆☆
Star Quality	★★★★☆

MARI

In a 2007 Japanese film, an abandoned dog is adopted by two sisters and named Mari before giving birth to three puppies. The film about their life, *A Tale of Mari and Three Puppies*, centres around the 2004 earthquake in Japan and how the dogs save their adoptive family. A big hit, it grossed over £20m ($30m) and, in a reversal of the norm, has led to a novel of the story.

Shiba Inu

Fame	★★★☆☆
Heroism	★★★★☆
Films	★☆☆☆☆
Recognition	★★★☆☆
Star Quality	★★★★☆

Fame	★★★☆☆
Heroism	★★★☆☆
Films	★★☆☆☆
Recognition	★★☆☆☆
Star Quality	★★★★☆

Mastiff-Labrador Retriever cross

SPIKE

Not the most prolific performer, Spike played the iconic role of loyal dog Old Yeller in the 1957 Hollywood film of that name – a classic for dog lovers everywhere and a guaranteed tear-jerker. A rescue dog, Spike was trained by Frank Weatherwax, who was well known for training Pal, the original dog to play Lassie.

St. Bernard-Scotch Shepherd cross

BUCK

The *Call of the Wild*, 1903, a novel by American author Jack London, describes the journey of Buck, set against the backdrop of The Klondike Gold Rush in 1890s Canada. To survive, he has to drop his domesticated airs and rediscover his more primitive instincts. The novel has been adapted for the big and small screen, the first time in 1923 and recently in 2020. London's *White Fang* is a reverse story, showing a wild wolf-dog's passage into civilization.

Fame	★★★★☆
Heroism	★★★★☆
Films	★★☆☆☆
Recognition	★★★☆☆
Star Quality	★★★☆☆

TOTO (TERRY)

Terry's life and name changed when the six-year-old was cast as Toto in *The Wizard of Oz* in 1939. Owned by celebrity trainer Carl Spitz, she only just made it to the end of the yellow brick road after breaking her foot, but just two weeks later she was back on set earning her weekly $125. The fame brought by the film led to her changing her name from Terry to Toto.

Fame
Heroism
Films
Recognition
Star Quality

RIN TIN TIN

The first canine superstar was rescued from the World War I battlefields in France by US Army Corporal Lee Duncan. Rin Tin Tin gained his first starring role in *Where the North Begins* in 1923. The film is credited with helping Warner Brothers avoid bankruptcy. Myth has it that Rinty was voted best actor in the 1929 Oscars, but the Academy forced a re-vote and he lost to German actor Emil Jannings. When he died in 1932, newspapers printed obituaries.

Fame
Heroism
Films
Recognition
Star Quality

BELLE

French actress-turned-author Cécile Aubry's children's book *Belle and Sebastian* was adapted for a television series shortly after publication in 1965. The novel's plot sees Belle and six-year-old boy Sebastian try to stop Nazi troops capturing French partisans. Aubry wrote and directed some episodes and her son played Sebastian. A Japanese animated TV series based on the story, *Meiken Jolie*, has also been produced, along with films and further series.

Fame	★★★★☆
Heroism	★★★★☆
Films	★☆☆☆☆
Recognition	★★★★☆
Star Quality	★★★★☆

Great Pyrenees

COOK

Born Lucke in 2000, Cook found fame as the star of Spanish Lottery adverts playing Pancho. In 2010, wearing a tuxedo, he attended the Goya Awards, the Spanish Oscars. His Pancho character was so popular that a film was written especially for him. *Millionaire Dog*, about a dog who has won the lottery, was released in 2014.

Jack Russell Terrier

Fame	★★★★☆
Heroism	★★☆☆☆
Films	★★★☆☆
Recognition	★☆☆☆☆
Star Quality	★★★★★

SKIPPY

Like Toto, Skippy became synonymous with his most famous role, Asta (The Pooch), in the 1934 comedy thriller *The Thin Man*. Starring Myrna Loy and William Powell, the film was so popular that it generated five sequels, of which Skippy appeared in three. His other hit was with Cary Grant and Katherine Hepburn in *Bringing Up Baby* (1938). The baby of the title was a leopard!

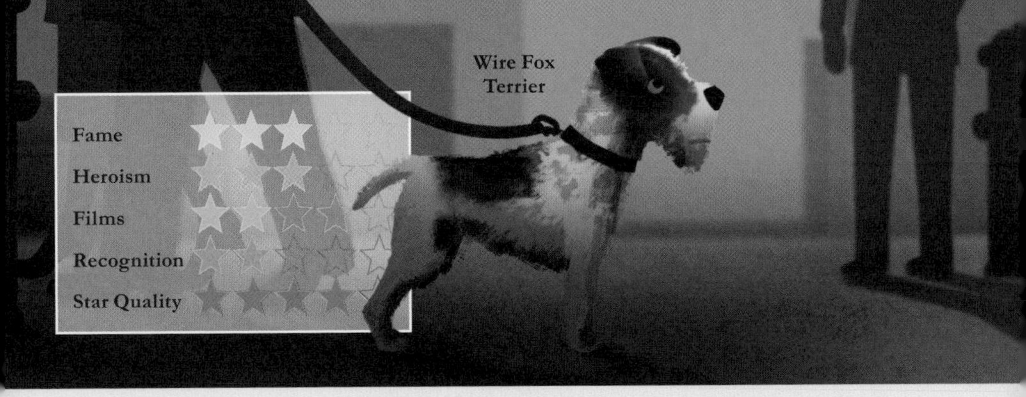
Wire Fox Terrier
Fame
Heroism
Films
Recognition
Star Quality

TOP OF THE PUPS

It's been impossible to separate the winners, so gold goes jointly to Rin Tin Tin and Lassie who share the top spot, appropriately, in a photo finish. Walking the yellow carpet to pick up a bronze award is Toto.

Lassie
Rin Tin Tin
Toto
Belle
Buck

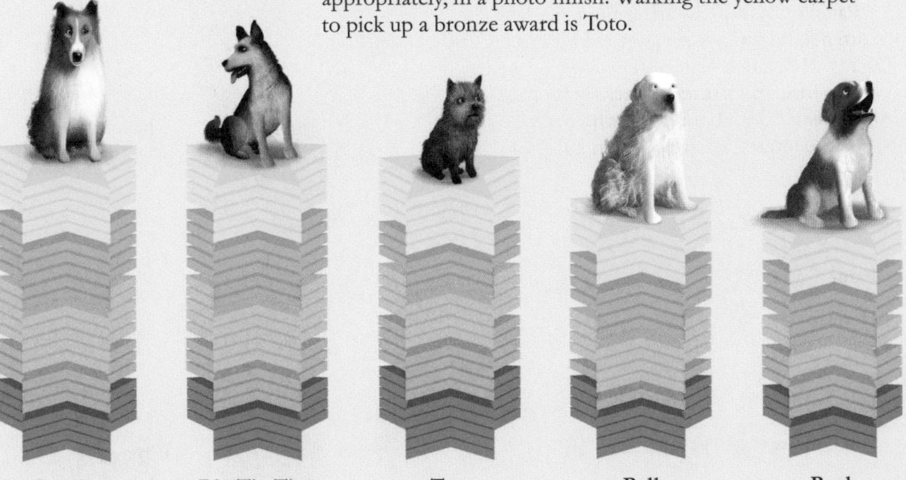

And then there were none

Like skirt lengths, hairstyles, and music, dog breeds come in and go out of fashion. Because pedigree dogs have their procreation controlled by humans, breeds can become extinct simply because they are no longer fashionable.

Kennel clubs around the world are much more aware of the possibility of this happening now and most hold a vulnerable breeds list to highlight breeds whose registration figures have dropped worryingly low. There is even a special category at Crufts for vulnerable breeds to raise awareness, but here we look at a few breeds for whom this action came too late.

Alpine Spaniel

It is no surprise that the Alpine Spaniel appears in the family tree of the St. Bernard. The breed was maintained by monasteries in the Alps to seek out lost trekkers in bad weather. Working in pairs, they would find people in trouble and lead rescuers to save stricken folk. The treacherous work carried out by the Alpine Spaniel put the

Alpine Spaniel

Turnspit Dog

breed at risk. It was finally brought to extinction near the mid-19th century due to the spread of disease through the region. The line lives on in the St. Bernard, named after an Alpine pass, and in the Clumber Spaniel. The latter is a mix of the Alpine Spaniel and the Bassett Hound.

Turnspit Dog

How would a modern Kennel Club classify the Turnspit Dog? Surely as a working dog, for it was occupied in kitchens in a treadmill used to turn the spit roast. It is hard to think of a more specific and limited role and therefore it is not surprising that the breed is now extinct. The height of the Turnspit was the middle 1800s when it spent its time in a wheel, not dissimilar to those you see in mouse cages. The wheel was attached to the spit roast placed in front of a roaring fire, and an even cook was ensured by the dog's efforts.

Moscow Water Dog

Red Star Kennels, the Soviet state-run organization set up to provide dogs for the military services, bred the Moscow Water Dog from various shepherd dogs. Its hoped-for occupation was to have been rescuing personnel from the water. Sadly, the breed was not suited to the work, preferring to attack the men or women it was sent to save. Its development was halted before it was ever officially recognized as a breed.

Moscow Water Dog

Brazilian Tracker
Brazilian Tracker or Rastreador Brasileiro had only been recognized by the FCI in 1967 when shortly afterwards it was decimated by disease to such an extent that within six years it had been declared extinct. It was a hunting dog, using scent, and efforts have since been made, by a club set up for the purpose, to recreate the breed. The efforts of the club have been successful such that in 2013, the Brazilian Kennel Club recognized the breed as being extant again.

English Water Spaniel
The English Water Spaniel was around in Shakespeare's time, receiving a mention in *The Two Gentlemen of Verona* (c. 1590): "She hath more qualities than a water spaniel, which is much in a bare Christian." A hunting dog, it was last seen in the 1930s.

The rise in popularity of other water dogs, especially the Labrador Retriever, slowly led to the disappearance of this intelligent breed, although there are echoes of it in English and Welsh Springer Spaniels.

Old English Bulldog
John Scott's engraving of an Abraham Cooper painting, *Crib and Rosa*, has preserved the image of the Old English Bulldog, a breed developed specifically for bull-baiting. In 1835, the Cruelty to Animals Act was passed in Britain; the aim of which was to protect animals from maltreatment. The act specifically made it

Brazilian Tracker (Rastreador Brasileiro)

The English Water Spaniel

an offence to keep premises for the purposes of animal fighting. The act was successful but a side-effect was that the Old English Bulldog became extinct. This has happened to many of the early fighting breeds such as the Bullenbeisser. The breed lives on in its descendants, among which is the Old English Bulldogge (not a typo), which is recognized by the United Kennel Club in the United States.

Keeping count

The Kennel Club in the UK counts breeds as vulnerable if they have fewer than 300 registrations in a year. If they have fewer than 450 registrations they are classified "at watch". There are similar schemes all around the world to make sure that future editions of this book do not need a longer section on extinct breeds.

Old English Bulldog

Record breakers

Jamaican athlete Usain Bolt, the quickest man ever, would trail in the wake of Fanta, a Greyhound from Australia. Bolt's fastest recorded speed is 44.73 km/h (27.8 mph) during a 100-metre race in 2009, but that's only just over half the speed of Fanta's personal best.

WORLD'S FASTEST

Super-speedy Fanta the Australian Greyhound won 42 out of the 62 races she started. By the time she put her paws up in 2018, she had won her owner $1.4 million Australian dollars in prize money.

Fanta, Greyhound
81.3 km/h (50.5 mph)

BIGGEST LITTER

Tia, a Neapolitan Mastiff, had a single litter of 24 puppies. The vet had told her owners to expect eight puppies, perhaps ten, so it was a bit of a surprise when they just kept coming!

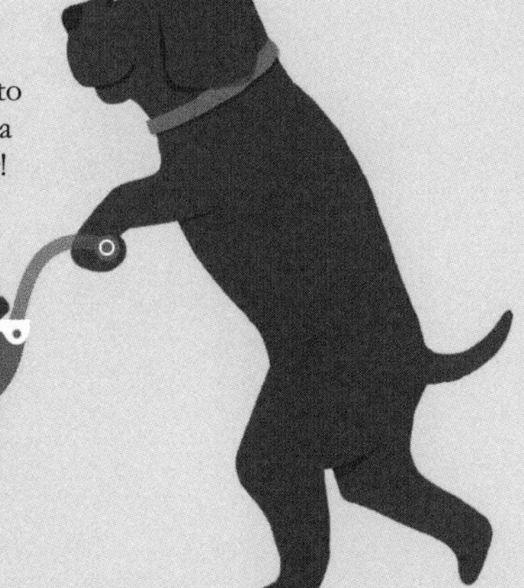

IT'S A DOG'S LIFE

Australian cattle dogs, such as old-timer Bluey, seem to be particularly long-lived. He worked on a ranch from 17 June 1910 to 14 November 1939.

Bluey, Blue Heeler
29 years and 160 days

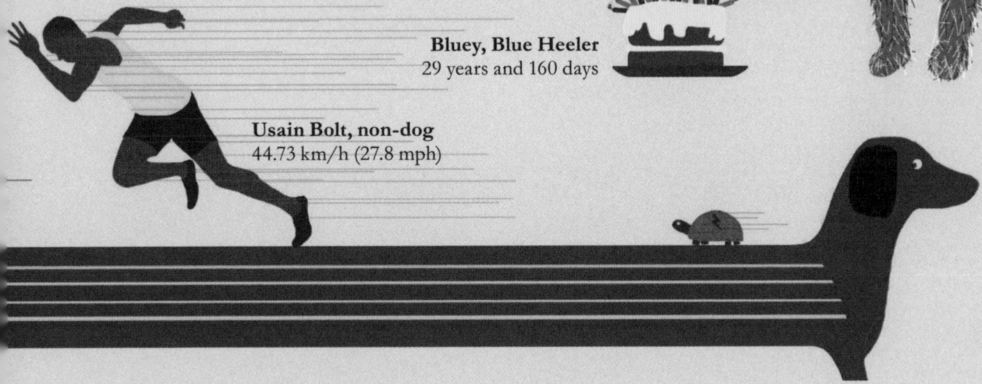

Usain Bolt, non-dog
44.73 km/h (27.8 mph)

EXTREME EXTREMITIES

Determined trackers with a keen sense of smell, Bloodhounds like Tigger are used by police forces all over the world because they keep their noses and long ears to the ground!

*This was Tigger's right ear, his left was only 34.2 cm (13.46 in)

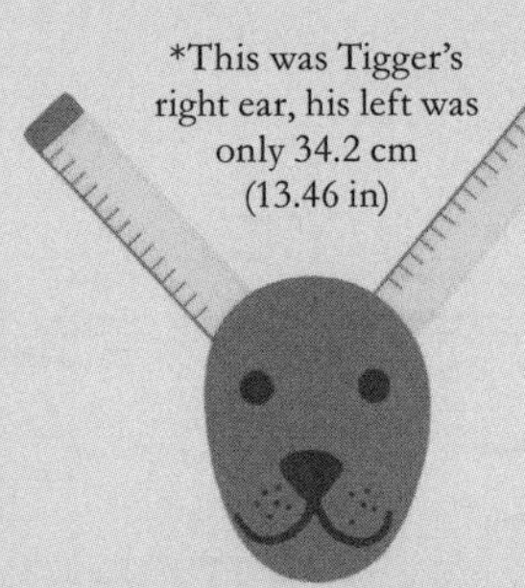

Longest ears
Tigger, Bloodhound
34.9 cm (13.74 in)*

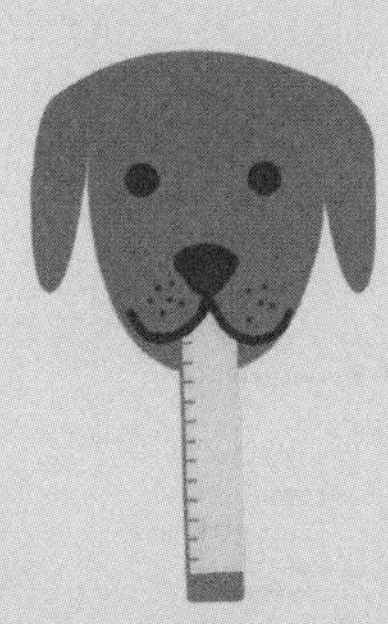

Longest tongue
Mochi, St. Bernard
18.6 cm (7.32 in)

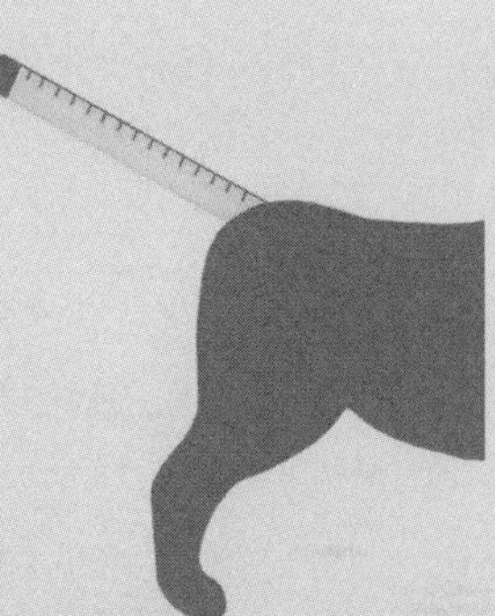

Longest tail
Keon, Irish Wolfhound
76.8 cm (30.23 in)

Dogs in law

Famously Mr Bumble in Charles Dickens' *Oliver Twist* states that "the law is an ass" and when it comes to dogs, in various parts of the world, it is hard to disagree. Some of these laws are meant for the protection of dogs, some are meant for our protection from dogs, but if sense were common, as it is meant to be, they probably wouldn't be needed.

What a stink!
We all know that dogs can, occasionally, get a little smelly but it would be best not to take your pongy pooch to New Castle, Delaware, USA. By-laws there define a dog as being a public nuisance if it, among other things, "creates an odour that is noxious or offensive or that constitutes a substantial annoyance, inconvenience, or injury to the public".

Dead wrong
The dog walking rules are quite tough all over the US with few places allowing off-lead walking, but in Hartford, Connecticut, it is illegal to walk your dog in a cemetery, even on a lead. Maybe they are worried about them digging for bones.

Rule of three
George Orwell's *Animal Farm* describes a world where the animals rule the world and maybe this is why in most parts of the US, groups of more than three dogs are not allowed to congregate on private property without a signed permit from the mayor. Who knows what they might get up to.

Walkies!
Unless you like lots of exercise it's best not to have a dog in Turin, Italy, where it is the law that they must be walked at least three times a day. It's slightly less taxing in Germany where walks must be twice a day.

Shhh!
Until 2007 it was forbidden, having been warned by a police officer, to incite your dog to bark in the Lancashire coastal town of Morecambe, England.

Regulated rest

If you want to buy a dog in Japan don't leave it too late in the day. Pet shops are only allowed to display them until 8pm, at which time the dogs are put to bed for 12 hours of beauty sleep.

Dog tax

Germany has a dog levy which varies depending on the size and type of the canine. The Hundesteuer is meant to discourage people from having too many dogs and also helps pay for services related to dogs.

Hanging offence

In the UK nothing is more important than the Royal Family, so it is no surprise that until 1965 it was a capital offence to allow your dog to mate with a dog from the Royal Household without permission, and presumably dinner.

Enlightened law

The Swedes take mental health very seriously and this extends to their dogs; who must have access to a view of a window allowing sunlight. Given that on average it is sunny 45 per cent of the time in Sweden, maybe they should issue sunglasses to all dogs.

Crufts

The first Crufts was in 1886 and was actually called First Great Show of All Kinds of Terriers. It wasn't until five years later that the show bore the name it now holds.

In 1891 Cruft's Seventh Great Dog Show was held at what would be its home until 1939, the Royal Agricultural Hall in London, and allowed all breeds to enter. Even so it wasn't until 1905 that the Best in Show was awarded. At this time it was referred to as Best Champion. The more familiar title didn't come into use till 1928.

The show is named after its founder Charles Cruft, he's listed as "Chas" on the inside cover of the first catalogue. His first involvement with the world of dogs was as an office boy and ultimately travelling salesman with the first dog food manufacturer, Spratt's. On his travels, which took him all over Europe, he had been invited to organize various dog shows and this led to that first show and eventually to what is known the world over as Crufts.

The show is currently held at the NEC in Birmingham where it has been since 1991. Prior to that it was at Earl's Court in London from 1979 to where it had moved the short distance from Olympia, its home since 1948.

An important landmark in the history of the show came in 1974 when it changed its name from Cruft's to Crufts. It had been decided that the apostrophe was no longer required in spite of the grammatical correctness of it.

Best in Show

Lots goes on at Crufts every year but the thing it is best known for is the ultimate prize of Best in Show. Only pedigree dogs can enter and there are strict breed standards. The route to the podium on the last day requires three rounds of competition. First of all there is the Best in Breed. The winners from that progress to Best in Group and then finally Best in Show. A second-placed dog is always selected and these are referred to as Reserve Best in Show.

Fifty-four per cent of winners have come from just two groups; Gundogs and Terriers. The oldest winner was Vbos The Kentuckian, a flat-coated Retriever, who was 9 years and 7 months when he won it in 2011. The youngest was Elch Elder of Ouborough. The only Great Dane to win Best in Show was two months shy of his second birthday when he towered atop the podium in 1953.

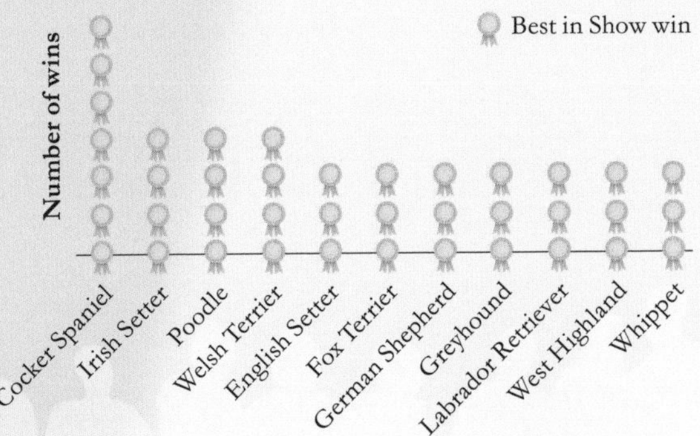

Best in Show by breed

Always the bridesmaid; Kerry Blue Terriers and Miniature Poodles have each been Reserve three times without ever winning Best in Show. The Cocker Spaniel is head and shoulders above any other breed when it comes to the title with seven wins. All but one of those was under the breeding of Mr H. S. Lloyd. His six titles give him twice as many as any other owner and he is responsible for three of only five dogs to have won the title more than once.

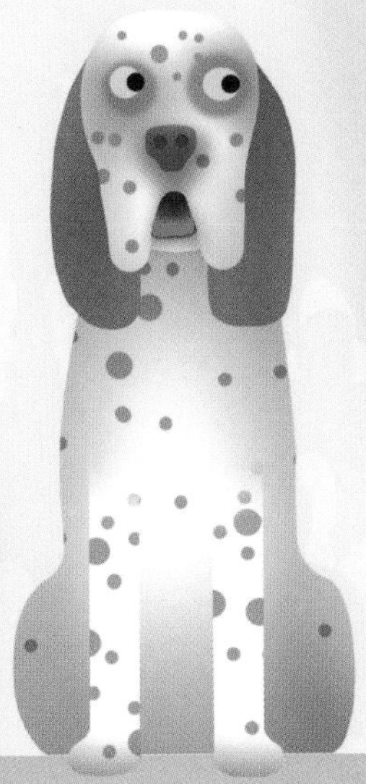

New competitions

Other than Best in Show and the levels below it, there are now various other competitions which take place. The first of these to be introduced was Obedience in 1955. That was it for more than 20 years before the floodgates opened: Agility was demonstrated in 1978 and competition held from 1980, Flyball arrived in 1990, and Heelwork to Music in 2005 following a number of years as a demonstration. Obreedience [sic] is a new addition to encourage other breeds to give Obedience tests a go. There are also competitions for Young Dog Handlers and for Gamekeepers.

The winning-most breeds in both Obedience and Agility do not come as much of a surprise.

Working Sheepdog

Border Collie

Belgian Shepherd (Tervueren)

German Shepherd

Australian Shepherd

Crossbreed

Dobermann

Golden Retriever

Poodle (Standard)

Obedience

Across various tests such as heelwork, recall, distant control, and retrieve, this competition tests how well a dog is trained to follow instructions. Working Sheepdogs top the winners' table by some margin.

Border Collie

Crossbreed

Shetland Sheepdog

Cocker Spaniel

Poodle (Miniature)

Working Sheepdog

Agility

This is basically an assault course for dogs, with the quickest around the course winning. The energetic and athletic Border Collie has the most wins.

Best in Group

The first year that the Best in Group was awarded was in 1956. Until then the breeds and groups had been judged, but simply as a way to narrow down the field for the best in show. In 1956 the groups were Hound, Gundog, Terrier, Toy, and Non-Sporting. In 1967, Non-Sporting was split into Utility and Working. The Pastoral group was introduced in the 1999 prizes to give us the seven groups we now have. This chart shows the five breeds that have won each group the most and how many times they have won.

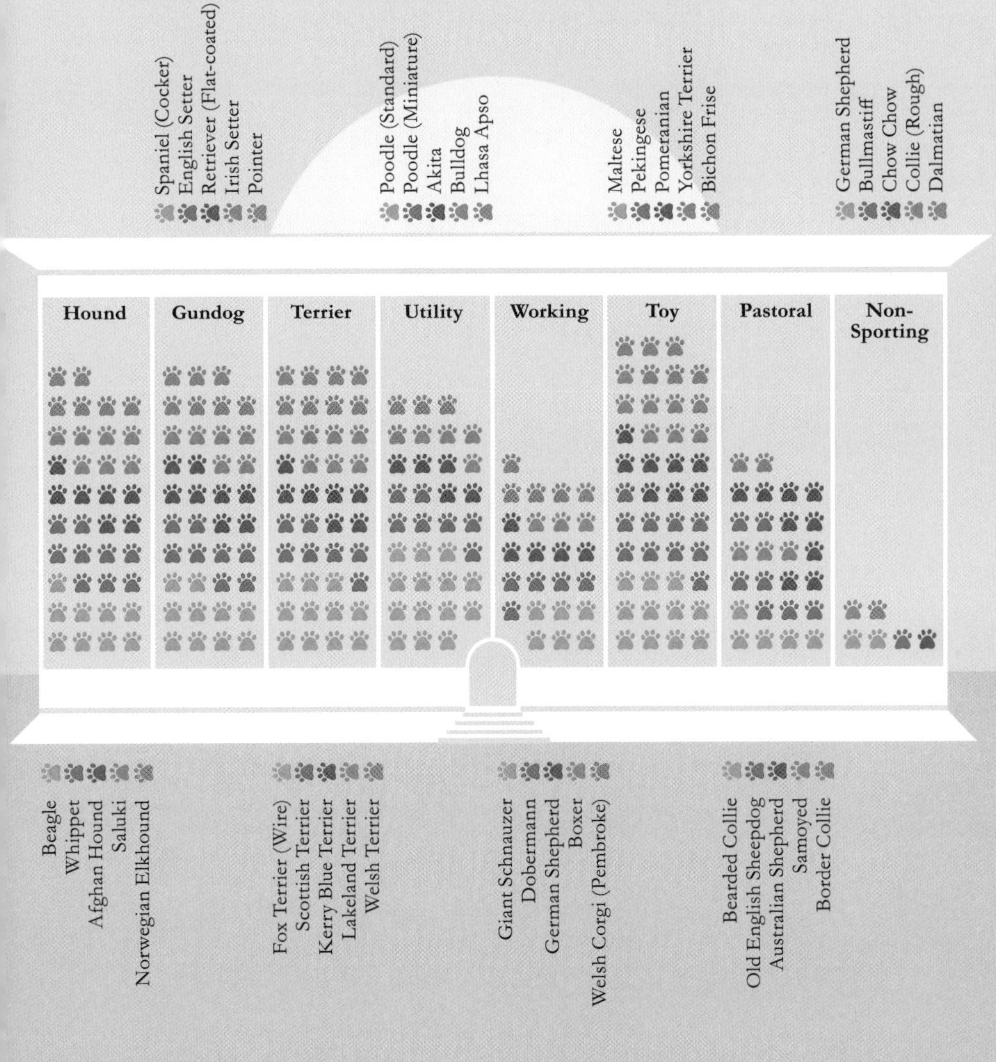

A dog's life

What makes a happy life? There is no accurate equation for this, but there are lots of numbers that make up the life of the average dog. Taking an average life expectancy of 11 ½ years, or 4,200 days – the time it takes Jupiter to orbit the Sun – for a dog weighing 20 kg (44lb), here are the vital statistics that add up to a life.

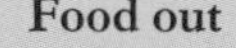

Food out

A dog will leave behind the equivalent of 21,000 oranges in poo.

Heartbeat

A dog's heart will beat around 544,320,000 times in its 11½ years.

Water out

Coming out the other end will be more than 52 bathtubs worth of pee.

Water in

In its lifetime a dog will drink more than 5,000 litres of water, which seems a lot, but is only 0.2 per cent of the capacity of an Olympic-sized swimming pool.

Food in

Eating just under 1 kg (2 lb) of food per day adds up, over a dog's lifetime, to the weight of an Asian elephant. You'd need a big bowl for that.

Westminster Kennel Club Dog Show

In 1877, a full 14 years before the first official Crufts show, came the First Annual New York Bench Show of Dogs. It was presented "under the auspices" of the Westminster Kennel Club and was held at Gilmore's Gardens, which two years later became Madison Square Garden. Over 12,000 dogs were entered and it was so popular that an extra day, a fourth, was added to allow more visitors to see the dogs.

The Westminster Kennel Club started out as a means to help its members work their dogs "in the field", specifically hunting. It developed into an organisation intent on promoting responsible ownership and preserving breed standards. The club maintains its roots in sporting dogs by awarding trophies at the AKC Pointing Breed Gun Dog Championships.

The first Best in Show was awarded in 1907 and went to a Smooth-Haired Fox Terrier named Warren Remedy. She won it for the next two years too!

Best in Show
By far and away the leading breed in Best of Show is the Wire Fox Terrier with 15 wins. Five of the top 10 breeds are Terriers.

Multiple winners

Owned by socialite Winthrop Rutherfurd, Warren Remedy remains the only three-time Best in Show winner. The last time there was a multi-year winning streak was when an English Springer Spaniel called D.J. won Best In Show in 1971 and 1972.

Other competitions

The Junior Showmanship has run from 1934 and encourages the participation of young dog handlers up to the age of 18.

An Agility event was introduced in 2014 and allows mixed-breed dogs to compete. Contestants have to run, jump, and weave around obstacles, racing against the clock. So far all but one year has been won by Border Collies, the exception being an Australian Shepherd named Holster in 2016.

The Obedience competition was introduced in 2016. Maybe unsurprisingly they have all been won by a Labrador Retriever, in fact by the same one – the paradoxically named, in light of its wins, Rhumbline's Once In A Blue Moon.

Best in Show wins by group
Terriers top the Best In Show table, with Sporting dogs a distant second. The Herding group was a relatively recent addition, so there's no wonder it brings up the rear.

Best in Group

Best in Group has been awarded since 1924, with Hounds added in 1930 and Herding dogs in 1983. Greyhounds top the Hound group but have never gone on to win Best in Show, while every one of the four times the Airedale has topped the Terrier group it has gone on to win Best in Show. This chart shows the five breeds that have won each group the most and how many times they have won.

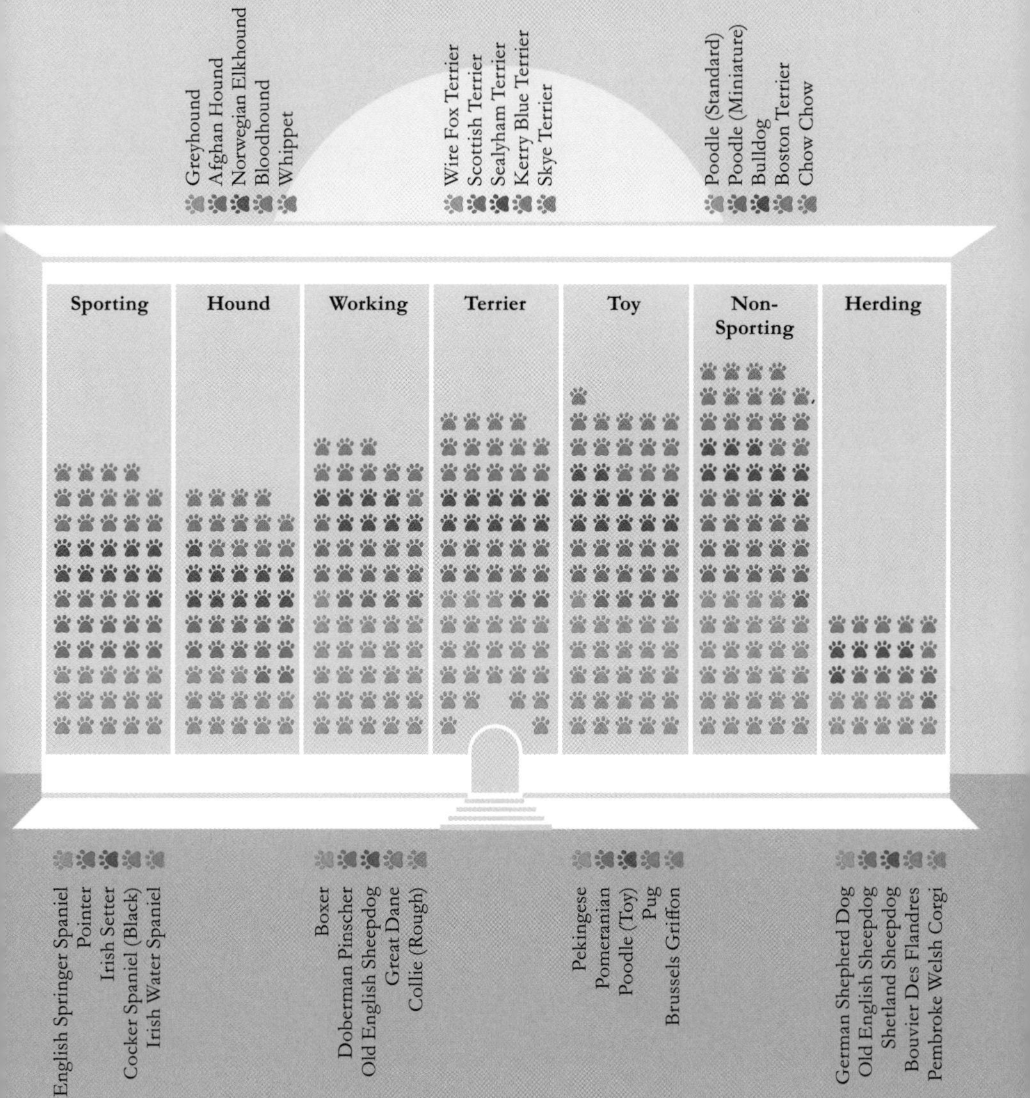

Greyhound
Afghan Hound
Norwegian Elkhound
Bloodhound
Whippet

Wire Fox Terrier
Scottish Terrier
Sealyham Terrier
Kerry Blue Terrier
Skye Terrier

Poodle (Standard)
Poodle (Miniature)
Bulldog
Boston Terrier
Chow Chow

Sporting
Hound
Working
Terrier
Toy
Non-Sporting
Herding

English Springer Spaniel
Pointer
Irish Setter
Cocker Spaniel (Black)
Irish Water Spaniel

Boxer
Doberman Pinscher
Old English Sheepdog
Great Dane
Collie (Rough)

Pekingese
Pomeranian
Poodle (Toy)
Pug
Brussels Griffon

German Shepherd Dog
Old English Sheepdog
Shetland Sheepdog
Bouvier Des Flandres
Pembroke Welsh Corgi

Great and small

Of all the animals in the world, the dog family has the greatest variation in size – and these records prove just that. Just look at tiny Milly standing next to donkey-sized Zeus! If humans had variation on the same scale, the tallest person in the world – based on dog extremes – would be nearly 6.4 m (21 ft).

Heaviest and lightest
The mighty Zorba stood almost 1 m (37 in) at the shoulder, and was 2.5 m (8 ft 3 in) long. A carefully placed paw would send the featherweight Ducky flying. Please note – no animals were harmed in the making of this comparison!

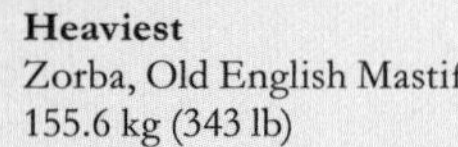

Heaviest
Zorba, Old English Mastiff
155.6 kg (343 lb)

Lightest
Ducky, Chihuahua
0.635 kg (1.4 lb)

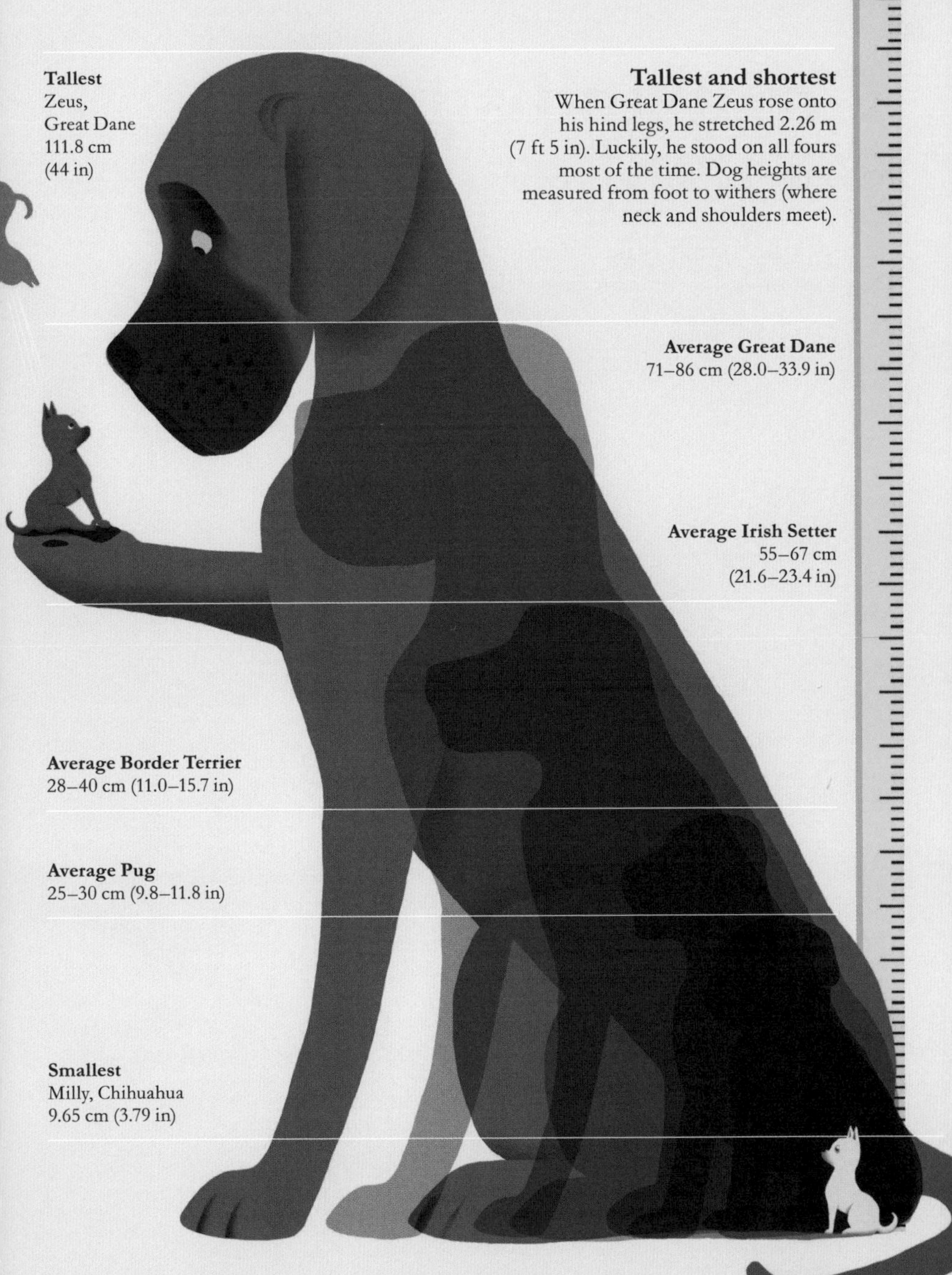

Tallest
Zeus,
Great Dane
111.8 cm
(44 in)

Tallest and shortest
When Great Dane Zeus rose onto his hind legs, he stretched 2.26 m (7 ft 5 in). Luckily, he stood on all fours most of the time. Dog heights are measured from foot to withers (where neck and shoulders meet).

Average Great Dane
71–86 cm (28.0–33.9 in)

Average Irish Setter
55–67 cm
(21.6–23.4 in)

Average Border Terrier
28–40 cm (11.0–15.7 in)

Average Pug
25–30 cm (9.8–11.8 in)

Smallest
Milly, Chihuahua
9.65 cm (3.79 in)

The World Dog Show

For nearly 80 years Crufts and Westminster were the two biggest dog shows in the world, but in 1971 they were joined by The World Dog Show. Organized by the Fédération Cynologique Internationale, the idea was to have a show that travelled the world and give every country a chance to host the planet's most amazing dogs.

That first show was in Budapest, Hungary, and the show has returned there twice. Dortmund in the west of Germany has been the host with the most having welcomed The World Dog Show four times. Amsterdam and Mexico City have both been the centre of the dog world three times, while 20 cities from Acapulco to Verona have put the benches up once making the show a very well-travelled beast indeed. And it is quite a beast with entries from all over the world hitting the 20,000 mark.

The thing that makes The World Dog Show special is that these dogs do come from all over the world. The winners have come from 20 different countries, while at Crufts and Westminster the Bests in Show are dominated by the home nation. Italy and the United States both boast eight winners each.

As with its senior equivalents in New York and the UK, The World Dog Show also showcases the things dogs do as well as simply how they look and perform in the parade ring, with prizes awarded in agility, obedience, and junior handling.

Top breeds
Beyond the success of the Saluki, the competition's top prize has been spread around quite evenly with perhaps a slight leaning towards the larger breeds.

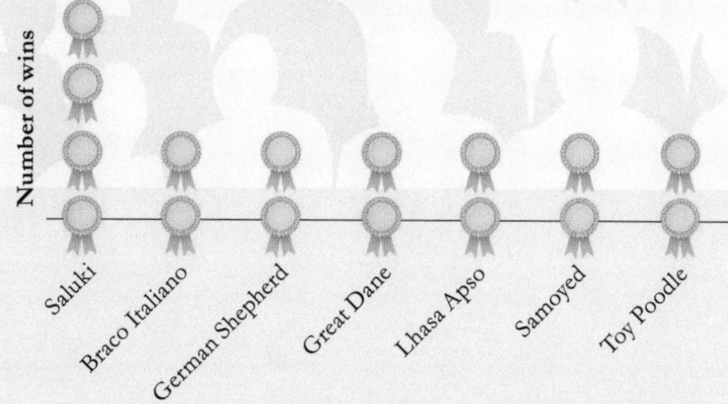

Saluki success

No Saluki has ever won at Crufts or Westminster, but the breed stands supreme at the World Dog Show with twice as many wins as any other breed.

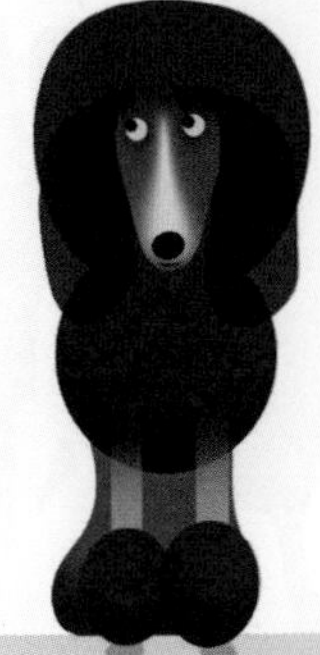

Awards

As well as its mobile nature, the other element that sets The World Dog Show apart is that it does not award Best In Show. Nothing so mundane for the "most important dog show in the world" (sic). Dogs from the four corners of the world compete for the Certificat d'Aptitude au Championnat International de Beauté, which translates as Certificate of Aptitude for the International Beauty Championship, or CACIB for short.

Since 1971 the CACIB has been awarded 44 times. The 2019 winner (the 2020 show was postponed due to Covid-19) was Realline Final Boss, a Welsh Corgi (Pembroke) from South Korea. It was the first winner from the breed. One breed has trotted off with the title four times – the Saluki – six have won it twice, and 28 breeds have won it once each. Maybe it is the nature of a travelling show and local judges that mean there has been no real dominance. Even in the FCI Groups the wins have been fairly evenly spread, with half the groups winning six or more times. The only group with no wins is FCI Group 4, but this is just Dachshunds so maybe not such a surprise.

Only three dogs have won the CACIB twice: Abrisa vom Felsenkeller, a Saluki from Germany in 1985 and 1986, Northwind's Rising Star, a Samoyed from the US in 1987 and 1988, and Smash JP Talk About, a Toy Poodle from Japan in 2007 and 2010.

Wins by country

No local bias is evident here as the title simply goes to the best dog, wherever they are from. Finland, Hungary, Norway, Portugal, South Korea, and Sweden have also won once.

Group winners

This chart shows the breeds that have two or more wins in the Best in Group rounds from 2000 to 2019.

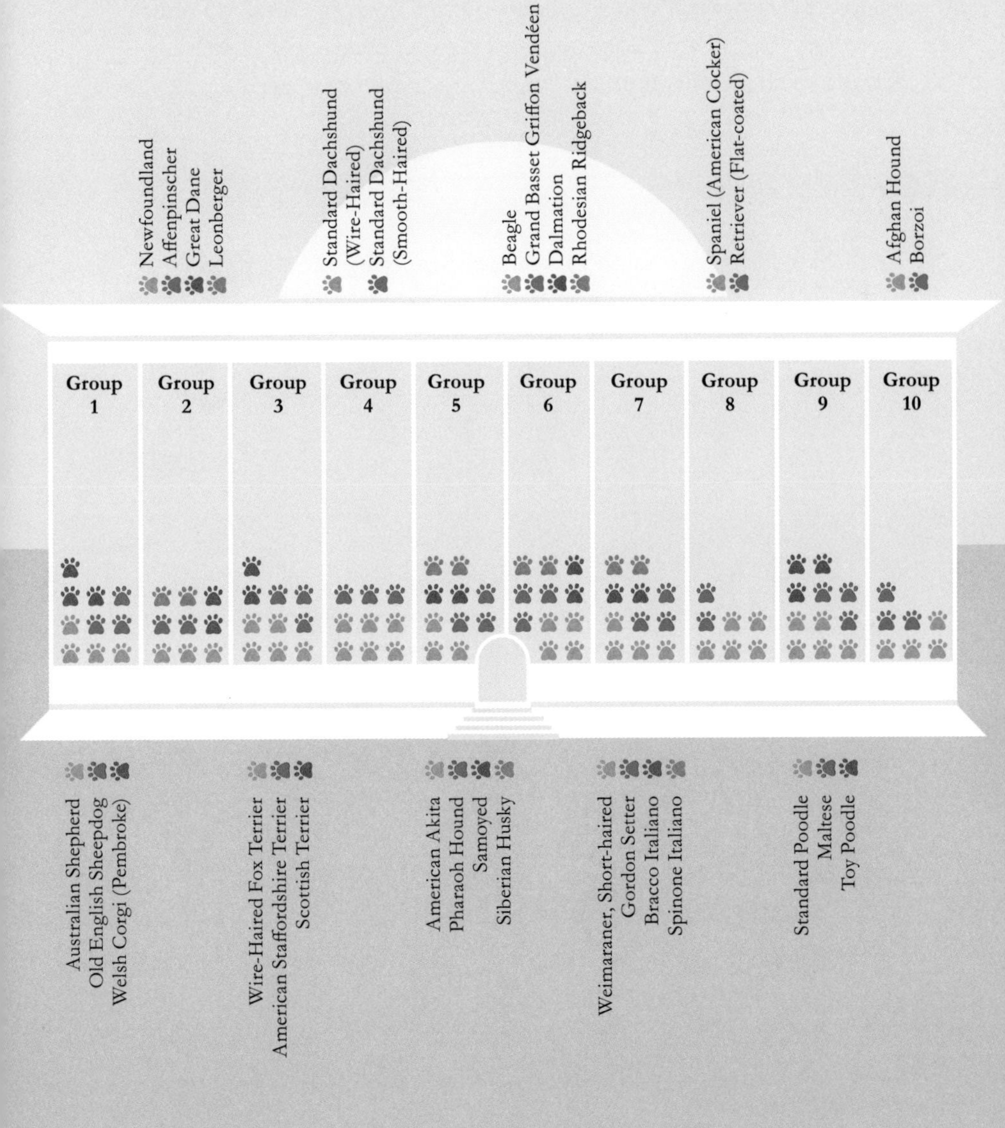

Choosing a dog

One of the reasons so much value is put on purebred dogs is that you know what you're going to get. The same as when you go to your favourite restaurant and pick a certain dish it will always be the same. Yummy.

Things to consider

Choosing a dog is still a difficult decision and this chart attempts to help by illustrating the six main things to think about and pointing the potential puppy parent in the right direction.

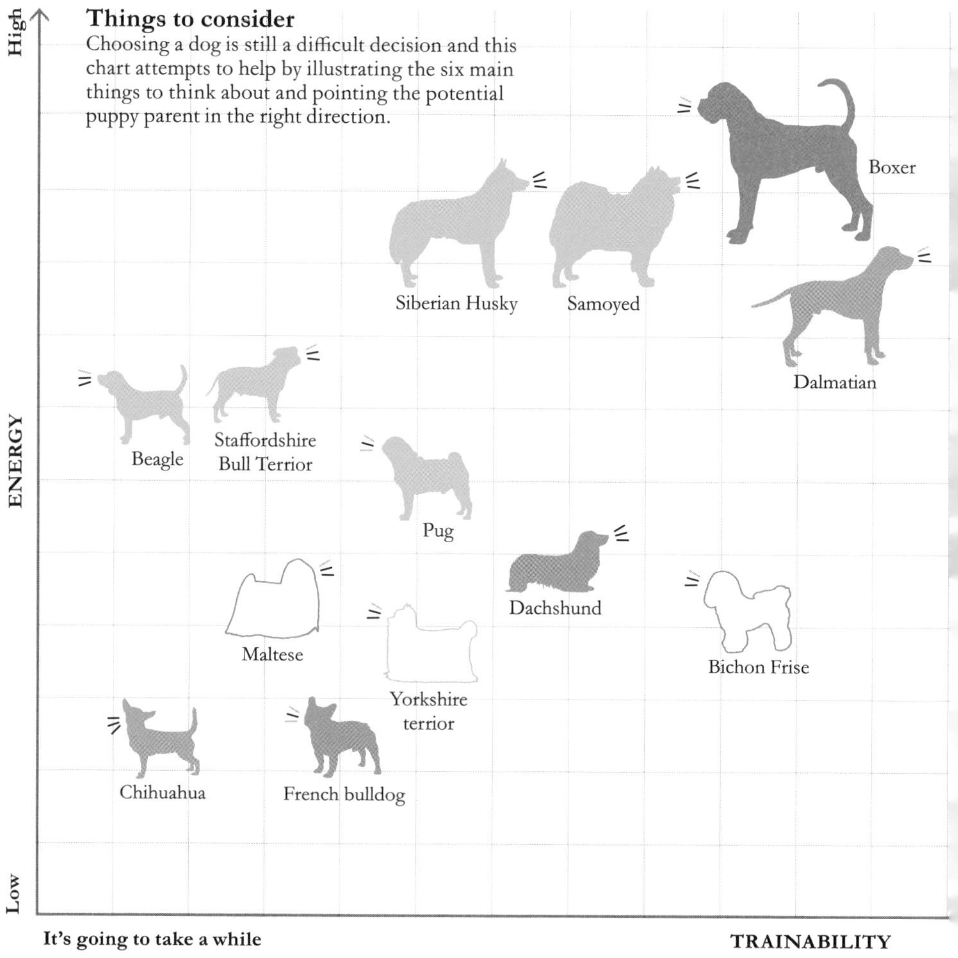

High

ENERGY

Low

Boxer

Siberian Husky

Samoyed

Dalmatian

Beagle

Staffordshire Bull Terrior

Pug

Dachshund

Maltese

Bichon Frise

Yorkshire terrior

Chihuahua

French bulldog

It's going to take a while

TRAINABILITY

KEY

Temperament

- Outgoing
- Friendly
- Alert/responsive
- Reserved with strangers

Sheds hair

- Yes
- No

Noise level

- Quiet
- Vocal
- Buy earplugs

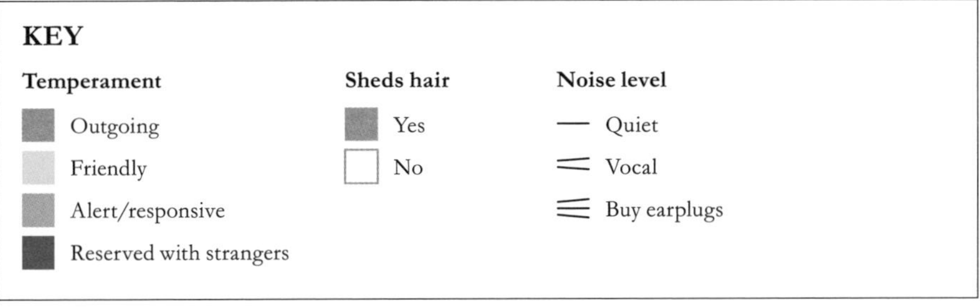

Labrador Retriever
Welsh Corgi (Pembroke)
German Shepherd
Poodle (Standard)
Border Terrier
Rottweiler
Cocker Spaniel
Miniature Schnauzer
Pomeranian
Easy peasy

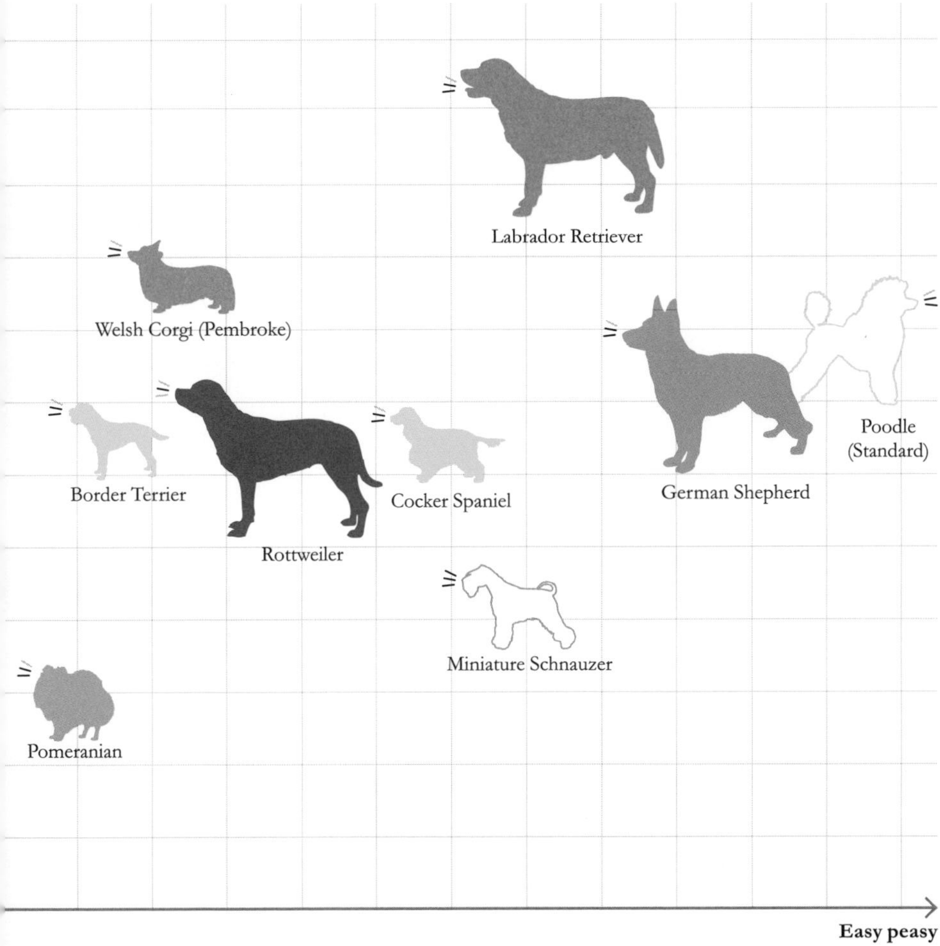

Glossary

Back
See Withers.

Beard
Thick, sometimes coarse and bushy hair around the lower facial area. Often seen in wire-haired breeds and their owners.

Bicolour
Any colour (except white) combined with white patches.

Blaze
Broad, white marking running from near the top of the head to the muzzle.

Blazer
Formal jacket worn by judges of dog shows.

Brisket
See Breastbone.

Breastbone
See Brisket. (Not to be confused with the famous horse Seabiscuit.)

Cape
Thick hair covering the shoulders. Not to be confused with cape worn by super heroes, although see Superdog (see pages 116–117).

Cat-like feet
Round, compact feet with the toes grouped closely together. Be careful, this may actually be a cat.

Croup
An area of the back just above the base of the tail. In some well-trained breeds this can be used as an occasional table.

Dewlap
Loose, hanging skin that falls in folds on the chin, throat, and neck of some breeds (for example, the Bloodhound). Can also be seen on some older dog owners.

Double coat
Coat consisting of a thick, warm underlayer and a weatherproof top layer. This does not refer to man-made coats, which dogs really shouldn't wear.

Gait
The way a dog moves.

Grizzle
Usually a mixture of black and white hairs, which gives a blue-grey or iron-grey shading to the coat. It is seen in some breeds of terrier.

Hackney gait
Dogs with this type of action, such as the Miniature Pinscher, raise the lower part of the leg particularly high as they walk.

Height
The distance from top of the withers to the ground.

Mask
Dark colouration on the face, usually around the muzzle and eyes. It could also be an actual mask.

Neck
See Withers.

Otter tail
A thickly furred, rounded tail that has a broad base and tapers to the tip; the hair on the underside is parted. It is seen in breeds such as the Labrador Retriever and Chesapeake Bay Retriever. It is also seen in many Otters.

Ruff
A long, thick collar of stand-out hair around the neck. One of the few words most dogs can actually say.

Saddle
A darker coloured area that cxtends over the back. Looks similar to a horse saddle.

Scissors bite
The normal bite of dogs. The upper incisors (front teeth) are slightly in front of but in contact with the lower incisors when the mouth is closed. The other teeth interlock with no gaps and form the cutting edge of the "scissors".

Shoulder
See Withers.

Spoon-like feet
Similar to cat-like feet (see page 156) but more oval in shape because the middle toes are longer than the outer toes. Be careful, this may be a cat, or even a furry spoon.

Topknot
Long tuft of hair on the top of the head. Became very popular with humans during the Covid-19 pandemic due to the closure of barber shops.

Topline
The outline of the dog's upper body from ears to tail. The opposite of bottomline.

Withers
The highest point of the shoulder, where the neck meets the back.

Index

R

S

T

U

V

W

Acknowledgements

Dorling Kindersley would like to thank Dr Sarah Morgan for veterinary advice, Joy Evatt for proofreading, and Helen Peters for the index.

The publisher would like to thank the following for their kind permission to use data supplied by them or sourced from their websites: American Kennel Club; Australian National Kennel Council Ltd.; Clube Português de Canicultura; Dutch Kennel Club "Raad van Beheer"; Japan Kennel Club (Mitsuo Miura); Korea Kennel Federation (Hyelin Kim); The Kennel Club (Ciara Farrel and Anna Kralova); The Westminster Kennel Club (Gail Miller Bisher).

Note from the author: I'd like to thank everyone at DK who has worked on this book. Firstly Stephanie Milner for making the vital introduction to Fran Baines who first said she liked my idea and on to Liz Wheeler and Karen Self who saw it over the line. In no particular order the rest of the team are: Kit Lane, Phil Letsu, Georgina Palffy, Amy Child, Julie Ferris, and Angeles Gavira. Thanks to David for bringing my words to life. Much gratitude to Ciara Farrell and Anna Kralova at The Kennel Club for opening up and digging in their archive for me. Also to Gail Miller Bisher at The Westminster Kennel Club for fact checking that section. Thanks also to Katie for putting up with me talking about the book every day for four years and finally, of course, to Rooney without whom none of this would have happened.